‘Rob Hamilton offers a differe. … question “Does God exist?” Instead of looking … around us and wondering whether we need to imagine a deity in order to make sense of it, he suggests flipping the question around and thinking about what it means to say that *anything* exists at all.’ Dr Martin Cohen, author of *101 Philosophy Problems*

Robert Hamilton

Anything Goes

A Philosophical Approach to Answering the God Question

Rough Bounds Communications

ISBN: 978-1-7385294-0-7 (paperback)
Published in 2024 by Rough Bounds Communications
With special thanks to Martin Cohen for advice and comments on the manuscript
For more, see www.anythinggoesmetaphysics.com

Anything Goes around here

Contents

Preface

The Map is not the Territory

Satnav plunges £96k Merc into river

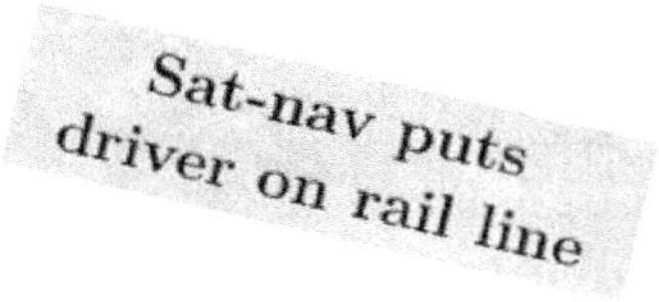
Sat-nav puts driver on rail line

Since GPS navigation systems became mainstream in the early 2000s, headlines such as “Satnav plunges £96k Merc into river” or “Sat-nav puts driver on rail line” have become commonplace. And who can help but smile when we come across these stories, despite the plight of the hapless individuals involved? The lesson we might draw from these parables is that ‘the map is not the territory’ – an old maxim that reminds us not to blindly follow advice without thinking about it. At a more abstract level, there could be said to be many ‘maps’ of the world at large – religions, philosophies or scientific models, each one claiming to give a description of how the world really is. And it is not surprising if we wonder whether any of these maps are any good. Is God, for example, a vital common reference point – or an optional decorative device? In the chapters that follow, I will present a new way of looking at age-old questions regarding the form of world around us and how much we can know about it, and in the process offer, I think, a distinctive new approach to perhaps the biggest question of all: “Does God exist?”

Questions regarding the form that the world around us takes, have been grouped by philosophers under terms such as Ontology or Metaphysics while considerations regarding how much – even in principle – we can know about this world is the branch of philosophy called Epistemology. There are various, and often competing, 'isms' or philosophical schools of thought on these issues, such as Scepticism, Realism, Anti-Realism, Foundationalism, Internalism, Externalism, Naturalism, Humanism, Materialism, Physicalism, Scientism etc. Under some schools of thought, God exists. Under some he doesn't. Under some, the question is unanswerable. I will argue that it *is* possible to reach a definitive answer to this question, and the purpose of this book is to take a curious lay reader, with no philosophical background, on a journey exploring the pertinent issues before then suggesting such an answer.

Our investigation will lead us into fields such as philosophy of religion, physics, neuroscience, philosophy of science and metaphysics. Inevitably it will not be possible to go into each of these subjects in great detail, but the aim is not to become an expert in each of these topics. And this is fine – one should not need a degree in philosophy in order to understand whether or not God exists! Rather, the aim is purely to gain a level of understanding that is sufficient to follow the overall line of reasoning, and avoid the spurious arguments, false trails and pitfalls that plague the more common arguments for and against God's existence.

PART I – SET UP

All the World is Models

Chapter 1

1. Who Cares whether God Exists?

Since time immemorial, humanity has had its gods. The ancient Egyptians had Osiris and Isis, the ancient Greeks had Zeus and the Vikings had Odin and Thor. The People of the Book (Jews, Christians and Muslims) have their one true God. As far as we know, all human societies evolved accompanied by gods of one form or another[i], yet since at least as far back as the ancient Greeks, the question of whether the Gods or God really exists has troubled mankind. Gods feature prominently in possibly the earliest text in western literature, the story of the Trojan War. We follow the fortunes of Greek heroes such as Achilles and Odysseus during the ten year siege of Troy, and the Gods are always there in the background, pulling the strings and determining the fates of the mortal protagonists. This story is told in the Iliad, believed to have been written down in c. 8th century BC. However, we also know that by the 5th century BC, philosophers in Greece were seeking natural explanations for celestial phenomena like thunder, rainbows and the movement of the stars. Protagoras, considered one of the leading intellectual of the time, said that he could not be sure that the Gods existed at all[ii]. And so for at least two millennia, debate about whether the Gods exist and the influence that they might have on mankind persisted unresolved.

Yet for many, the existence of God seems self-evident, both as an explanation for the events taking place around us, and as a source of spiritual guidance that gives our lives meaning. It has been widely accepted within Christianity for centuries that it is possible to come to know God directly, through prayer and meditation. Famous Christian mystics who, it is said, have experienced God in this way include Hildegard of Bingen and St. John of the Cross[iii]. And in the present day perhaps, there are also those who have had religious experiences whereby God's existence is so immediate, that he appears to them in the same way as do the sun and sky.

But for the rest of us, even those who practice their religion on a daily basis, there is doubt. Humanity appears to have always had its sceptics and the absence of concrete proof of his existence has always allowed atheists to argue that the events that unfold around us can be explained without the need for a supernatural deity. Indeed, since the Enlightenment, the march of science has increasingly provided us with detailed explanations for why crops fail or volcanos erupt, simply in mechanistic terms. In consequence, today for many, God appears increasingly surplus to requirements.

And so if the world can get by without God, then it seems increasingly plausible that there is no God. Yet in that case, what is it that gives our lives meaning? It is this question that haunts so many of us in the 21st Century. Within philosophy, the school of thought that insists that life is essentially meaningless is known as *nihilism* and many have made peace with this, finding a kind of freedom in the lack of obligation that it implies. Likewise, others have attempted to derive a moral code, not from religious doctrine, but from what we know about the world around us. A number of moral frameworks have been developed which proceed along these lines, for example, utilitarian or even hedonistic ones which derive an alternative morality based on what is important for us as human beings.

So why is it that one of these frameworks has failed to supplant religion as the primary moral code by which we all live today? The clue perhaps, is in the fact that 'a number' of such frameworks have been developed. While most of us will nod in agreement at Kant's advice to treat other people as 'ends' in themselves and not merely as a means to our ends, or more generally at Hippocrates' principle 'First, do no harm' , questions of morality are not always so simple. Most ethical questions involve balancing competing rights. For example, is it okay to steal if your family are starving? Should you save the life of your child or the lives of ten unrelated children? Ultimately, frameworks of this kind run into the 'Is-ought' problem, first identified by Scottish philosopher David Hume. This makes the point that it is not logically valid to derive an 'ought' statement from an 'is' statement. You cannot say 'because things are like this, I should do that' without including extra, value based, information in the premise. Let's take a seemingly uncontroversial statement like 'He killed another man, therefore he should go to gaol'. For this statement to be logically true, we need another premise; another rule to follow – for example 'the punishment for killing someone is gaol' – which is a value based premise. Otherwise, it takes for granted that killing deserves a punishment, and so implicitly assesses killing as wrong. Now, such assessments can be justified on a number of grounds. We can appeal to a sense of fairness and equity – you wouldn't like someone to kill you, so you shouldn't kill others. We can appeal to utility – you shouldn't kill because it will lead to great distress and hurt. Or we can take a more pragmatic view – if killing was acceptable, it could lead to everyone killing each other and there would be no-one left. However, despite all these arguments, most societies do permit killing in certain circumstances e.g. war or perhaps self-defence or the defence of others. And so, as Hume points out, whether killing is right or wrong is not a logical consequence of the facts of the situation. Rather, it involves making a call; making a judgement. And such judgements are subjective.

Of course, there is nothing stopping each of us from finding our own meaning in life and deciding on our own moral code. For you, the most important value may be 'the sanctity of life', for me, it might be 'happiness' or 'freedom'. Or perhaps 'spontaneity'. But with no common arbiter for values, such judgements about which values are the most important are subjective. And even if a common standard of values could be agreed, with no link to agreed facts about the world, such a standard would be arbitrary

– a rationale could be found for selecting a different set of values as primary.

And so many people, if they have their health and enough to eat, and their other immediate concerns are satisfied, find themselves asking 'Why am I here? What is it all for?' Science is very good at explaining the 'what', but there is a deafening silence when it comes to the 'why'.

As well as causing consternation at a personal level, the lack of clarity over God's existence is a well-known source of conflict within society. Without God to provide some meaning and guidance, what is the purpose of it all? Atheists may consider themselves to have transcended such questions, and to have a more modern view (although, as noted above, atheism has been around since at least the time of the ancient Greeks), yet others may describe atheism itself as a dogma, often held unreflectively. The atheist might say

"These believers are like children believing in unicorns or Father Christmas. We, on the other hand, have a grown-up approach and seek evidence before believing in fairy tales. Look at these idiots, believing in something for which there is no proof or even reliable evidence. It must be a sign of weakness. Unable to stand on their own two feet, they need someone to hold their hand through life".

To be sure, many believers find such talk patronising and insulting. After all, and at the very least, just as there seems to be no proof that God exists, there also appears to be no proof that God does not exist. At the other extreme, fervent believers may be suspicious of unbelievers or 'infidels', noting, as we have above, that without God, their values may be left ungrounded. What is to stop these people behaving however they like? The infidels may be able to justify their behaviour in their own minds, but is it good for society and in line with God's teachings? Liberal democracies often look to separate church and state, but in that case, on what basis are our laws of society grounded? Without 'God's guiding principles', we are left with the humanist views touched on above or social norms. Again, the lack of clarity provided here is a source of strong disagreement and conflict.

I put 'God's guiding principles' in inverted commas, because of course, who is to say what God's guiding principles are? Do we look to religious authorities? Or do we pray for guidance and listen to our hearts, perhaps? Cynics may claim that God's principles are surely human ones, dressed up as divine to provide them with a bit more authority. Do the ten commandments come directly from God or reflect social norms? And we can note that different religions make different and often contradictory claims about what God's guiding principles are. A topical example is the Taliban's policies on the education of women, which is very different to modern Christian policy. And of course, Christian policy towards women has itself changed over time. Is this because God's principles have changed?[iv] Today, violence in the name of religion remains a regular occurrence, with terrorist acts motivated by religious extremism perpetrated on a regular basis. And different religions – different world views – have vied for supremacy for centuries; examples include the Crusades between Christian and Islamic forces lasting from 1095 to 1291 AD and the earlier efforts by Christians to convert pagans.

If we were looking for religion to provide social leadership and a focal point for moral unity then perhaps it is not unfair to say that in the 21st century, the opposite is the case. Religion is often seen as a source of division, with the separation of church and state aiming to prevent any one religion holding sway over society.

And so, for all these reasons and more, the question of whether or not God exists remains central for us as individuals and for society as a whole. In exploring the answer to this question, our investigation will aim to provide a deeper understanding of the world in which we live and so allow for clarity in our personal beliefs as well as provide a firmer footing on which we can move forward as a society.

*

This book takes an unconventional approach to exploring and answering the question of whether or not God exists. The conventional approach might be said to start by considering our understanding of God; namely that he is an all-powerful, all-knowing and fundamentally good being that created the world around us. This god ensures that events unfold in line with a divine plan, and intervenes as necessary to answer prayer and grant miracles, including the miracle of eternal life. Theists insist that such a being exists, atheists insist that there is no such being and agnostics are not sure. How are we to decide who is right? Conventional arguments for the existence of God look to show that were it not for God, things could not be the way they are. God is required to kick-start the universe into being and there are many examples where it is asserted that God must have intervened to save that poor child from certain death. We shall take a brief look at the philosophical arguments in Chapters 2 and 3, but it is perhaps fair to say that most people regard such debates as inconclusive. Theists see the hand of God at work in day to day events and atheists do not. But ultimately, it seems impossible to establish beyond reasonable doubt whether there is a God playing a role in daily events. And so in the early 21st Century, the jury seems to be out. He may exist. He may not. It seems impossible to tell for sure.

I propose taking a different approach. Instead of looking at the world around us and asking whether it must be the case that God exists in order for it to be the way it is, we take a closer look at what it means to say that something exists at all. We will see that the problem is not merely that we do not have the tools to uncover whether or not God exists. Rather, I aim to show that it makes no sense to even ask the question! Importantly, this shouldn't be interpreted as saying therefore that God doesn't exist. I won't be arguing that the concept of God makes no sense. What we will see is that the existence of God is *subjective*. God may exist for you – as genuinely and as truly as anything else that exists – but equally, he may not exist for me.

Now of course there are many objects that we are very happy to say do exist. This book in front of you exists, whether this is in the form of a physical paper copy or within an electronic device. The building I am sitting in exists, the earth exists, stars and planets exist. The palm tree in the desert oasis exists. Or does it? Might it be a mirage? This one might take a little more investigating, but we can establish the truth, by going up to it and touching it. Once we have satisfied ourselves of the truth of such things, is that the end of the story? We might vaguely be aware of various Buddhist or Idealist philosophies that claim that all the world is an illusion. Perhaps nothing that we see around us really exists? Now this may well be the case within the context of these philosophies, but this doesn't really help us here. What we want to know when asking whether God exists, is whether or not he exists in the same sense that these other objects exist. That is to say, we want to know whether there is such a being as described above – a being that created the world, listens to prayer and grants life after death etc. This God that we described above is an idea – a concept – that we are all familiar with. What we want to know is, is there such a thing in the world, to which this concept corresponds? This is our normal definition of existence. Unicorns don't exist, because although we can understand the concept of a unicorn, there is no such thing in the world to which this concept corresponds. The difficulty with this approach, I will aim to show, is that God is a completely different kind of animal and so trying to apply this definition of existence doesn't work.

The problem is exposed once we recognise that our definition of existence – the correspondence between an idea and a real object – is itself an idea. This idea is so ingrained into our thinking in the 21st Century that it generally goes completely unchallenged. The idea is that the universe is structured in a certain way, as a configuration of real objects, behaving in line with certain laws. Through rigorous and painstaking investigation, it is asserted that we can gain ever more knowledge of that structure and its behaviour. However, as many philosophers have argued, this assertion is groundless. The difficulty lies in how it is possible to gain any knowledge of these 'real objects' to which our concepts are purported to correspond. Philosophers and scientists have long recognised that all of our knowledge of the world comes to us by virtue of our own experiences. This means that our understanding of the universe is based on what we can see, hear, touch, taste and smell. Now at this point it may be objected that surely we have theoretical insights as well? For example, we know that the earth has a solid core at its centre made primarily of iron and nickel, without ever having observed or sampled it. However, the point is that all our theoretical insights about the world start with the raw data. Information about Earth's core mostly comes from analysis of seismic waves and the Earth's magnetic field, which are observable more directly. And so ultimately we are limited by what we can infer based on the information we receive through our senses. We are limited by our humanity. We speculate on how the universe must be structured in order to produce the results we observe, but we have no 'God's eye view' giving us a direct sight of this structure.

And so we have no direct sight of the 'real objects' of the universe – for example, the 'real' book behind the image of the book generated by the brain. These proposed 'real objects' are actually just concepts and our understanding of them is inferred from what we do see around us. We will see in Chapter 4 how the brain conjures up the objects in our minds that we interact with, in order to make sense of the incoming data signals from our sense organs. We will see in Chapters 5 and 6 how scientists have conjured up all sorts of structures for the universe in order to make sense of experimental results. But if the problem of getting access to the 'real objects' of the universe is intractable, this casts doubt over the truth of the idea that there are 'real objects' out there to which our concepts correspond and that we can come to know. Philosophers have long recognised this, and have proposed alternatives to this dominant idea, which is generally termed scientific realism – broadly falling under the umbrella term of Idealism touched on above. Idealism is the idea that the world, or the world as humans can know it is fundamentally mental, mentally constructed or otherwise immaterial. This is perhaps a disconcerting idea to many. They might ask 'Am I just living in a dream world?' 'Is nothing I think I see actually real?' Some form of idealism has been advocated by Philosophers of the past, such as René Descartes, David Hume and Bishop George Berkeley and we will explore some of these ideas in due course. However, these alternative philosophies suffer from significant drawbacks of their own, not least the challenges raised above, and so these ideas are not mainstream today.

The case I am making in this book is that just because our brains conjure up certain objects, images for us to live by that might not be a true reflection of how the world actually is, *this does not mean that these objects and images are not real.* They are as real as anything can be. Without our brains making sense of all this incoming data, we would just have a kaleidoscope of colours, sounds, sights and smells. The brain takes this data and applies a coherent framework to it, forming a multitude of objects that we interact with, or to put it another way, a model of the world that we live by. Pythagoras is renowned for saying "All the world is numbers", but it would perhaps be more accurate to say "All the world is models". It is the model given to us by our brains that is familiar to us and allows us to make sense of the world. The objects given to us by our brains are analogous to the items we see on a map – they describe the territory of the world at large in a way that makes sense to us. However, when it comes to our conception of the universe, the map in our brains is all we have – we can never step beyond it and see the world as it really is. Nevertheless, we have been conditioned under the scientific realist idea to believe that there are 'real' tables and chairs out there, to which our sense impressions correspond, even if we cannot get direct sight of them. However, a moment's reflection allows us to realise that when we are considering tables and chairs, we are considering those objects as modelled by our brains. The true form of any 'real world' out there is beyond our comprehension – things only make sense to us in terms of how our brains model them. And so, I will argue, when we talk about tables and chairs, we can only be talking about features of our model. As far as each of us is concerned, this model or map *is* our world. It is the only world we can ever know and so contrary to popular belief, the map *is* the territory.

*

Now how does this help us understand whether God exists? Well under our correspondence definition of existence, we said that a thing exists if the concept of it corresponds to a 'real object'. But we then saw that 'real objects' can be no more and no less than the objects on our map. So when we are asking if God exists, we are looking to see whether our concept of

God corresponds to one of the objects on our map. Or to put it another way, we are looking to see if our map of the world – the universe as we see it – contains God.

This is revolutionary! Remember, we cannot step beyond our map to see the universe as it 'really is'. Everything we know, everything that has meaning for us, everything that makes sense to us, is on our map – the model that your brain puts together to assimilate all the incoming data in a way that makes sense to you. And so ultimately, I am arguing that the question of whether or not God exists boils down to this:

What does your model of the universe look like?

Does it contain a God? Does the universe make more sense to you with God in it? If so, then yes, he exists. If not, then no, he doesn't. God exists if you believe in him.

*

Now the first objection that may spring to mind at this point is 'But what if your model of the universe is wrong? What if you make sense of the incoming data through the idea that God doesn't exist, but actually it turns out that he does?' This is a confusion that results from the scientific realist way of thinking that has been ingrained into us since birth, but is actually completely groundless. It takes for granted the idea that not only is the universe structured in a way that can make sense to us in principle, but also that we as humans, have the capacity to comprehend this structure. This is a truly heroic claim to make, given that it is made purely on faith! In the next few chapters, we'll spend some time exposing just how dubious and dogmatic this claim is. Other metaphysics are available.

Chapter 2

2. The Triumph of the Sceptic

Throughout the ages, many learned and respected figures have energetically made the case for the existence of God. In this section, we will briefly go through three of the most well-known arguments. It may not come as a surprise to discover that most people do not find them particularly convincing. After all, we might expect that if they were, then the rationale for God's existence would be taught in all schools and be a well-established component of society's body of knowledge! Instead, these arguments seem to live on primarily as abstract philosophical relics. However, it will be helpful for later to go over what has been said. I will also touch upon a couple of the more modern approaches.

The Design Argument

The first argument we'll consider is the Design Argument. It essentially says that the universe is so well structured and organised that it could not possibly have just happened by chance. There must be some intelligence or *designer* behind it – and the only designer capable of this is God[v].

The central idea can be traced back to the writings of the satirist Lucian, in the 2nd century AD and goes back to Plato's Laws. But perhaps the most evocative account came in 1802 from William Paley, a British clergyman, in his book *Natural Theology or Evidences of the Existence and Attributes of the Deity*. Here, Paley uses the analogy of a watch, with the motions of the stars and planets compared to the moving clockwork parts of the mechanism. Just as a watch is designed by a watchmaker, so too must the universe be designed by a 'divine watchmaker'. The powerful idea is that it is as ridiculous to imagine the universe having formed the way it did by chance, as it is to imagine throwing springs and cogs into the air and having them land as a fully formed watch. Life, as well, shows signs of intelligent design, or so the argument runs. What is the chance of mixing up some chemicals in a primordial soup and a frog or a human crawling out?

Of course, in the 21st century, we have a one word reply – 'Evolution!' The theory of evolution explains how random variation between the generations, can lead, via natural selection, to creatures so well adapted to their environment, that it gives the appearance of conscious design. It is only the apparently 'well designed' creatures that are left in the world because those that resulted from a less suitable random variation did not survive. However the advocate of the Design Argument is not finished yet. They want to know how it is, not just that life forms seem to be designed, but why it is that the universe in general gives the appearance of design? Do the planets revolving around their stars, and stars revolving around the galaxies not bring to mind the cogs and hands of a clockwork watch? The atheist will respond that these are just the result of matter obeying the laws of nature following the Big Bang. But then, aren't the laws of nature themselves conveniently well ordered? Surely the laws of nature themselves, must have been designed to produce the delicate and extraordinary environment where planets can form and life can evolve?

However, it is possible to respond to this point in the same way as before. The universe does not have to have been designed; it could be the result of random variation. Perhaps it is just luck, that the universe is able to facilitate the development of life. Or perhaps there are lots of universes, with all sorts of randomly different laws of nature. We are lucky enough to find ourselves in one of only a small few of them that happen to be governed by stable, well-ordered laws. How to explain such extraordinary luck? Well, given the fact of our existence, it must be that we are in a well-ordered universe because without this order, we would not be around to observe it.

A second criticism, put forward by David Hume, is that even if the universe did have a designer, that designer need not have been the Christian God. This god is an all-powerful entity that is also the perfect Good, a god that responds to prayer and can grant life after death. A designed universe may suggest the need for an all-powerful designer (though it can be debated whether this only provides evidence for a *sufficiently* powerful designer, rather than an *all*-powerful designer). However, it doesn't seem to provide any evidence for a designer who has any moral leanings, least of all interest in human affairs, one way or the other.

The Cosmological Argument

If the Design Argument looks to God to explain the existence of order in the universe, the Cosmological Argument looks to God to explain how there came to be any universe at all. It is perhaps human nature to continually seek explanations, as we often observe with small children. Where do I come from? Where do babies come from? Where does the earth come from?

We can keep going back in time but when we get to the question 'Where does the universe come from?', it is not clear where we go from there. Modern physics tells us that the universe started with the Big Bang around 13.8 billion years ago, but offers only silence on what came before. The cosmological argument essentially says that given that there was no universe before the Big Bang, it can only have been created by God.

There are several objections that a sceptic could make to this claim, so let's touch on a few of them. The first objection might be in line with Hume's objection to the Design Argument, namely to ask why does this First Cause have to be God? Conventionally, we understand God as an infinitely powerful, infinitely knowledgeable and infinitely good being. But it is not clear that the cause of the universe needs to be a conscious being at all, let alone that this being needs to be in any way moral. In fact, for centuries, theologians have wrestled with what is known as 'the Problem of Evil", the point that the amount of evil in the world seems to be at odds with the idea of it being created and regulated by an ultimately good being. But let's say, for the sake of argument, that the universe was created by a supernatural power. What reason do we have to believe that that supernatural power is still around today?

In recent years, some physicists and philosophers have also raised the possibility that there may be much more to the universe than is conventionally taught. They point out, for example, that although the Big Bang was the beginning of the universe as we know it, this does not have to mean that it was the beginning of everything. It has been hypothesised that our universe is one amongst many, part of a so called 'multiverse', in which universes, perhaps like our own, pop in and out of existence at random. These universes may expand, but then reach a point where gravity pulls the universe back together again. It contracts until it is again so small that it explodes again in another Big Bang event. This cycle may perhaps repeat indefinitely, or at least could have happened in the past[1].

However, for the proponent of the Cosmological Argument, physical explanations for the beginning of our universe do not address the fundamental issue. Suppose for example that the Big Bang was caused by a random quantum fluctuation in the multiverse or perhaps a universe in its previous incarnation. In these cases, we can just ask 'well, what caused *that*?' It seems that eventually, you will have to get to, if not God, then some kind of supernatural explanation, because for every natural explanation, you can continue to ask what caused it, which is a process without end.

Even so, it is not clear that a supernatural explanation resolves the issue. Firstly, could someone not reasonably ask 'What caused God?' Was it

[1] Current thinking is that our universe is expanding too rapidly for gravity to be able to pull it back together and as such it will continue to expand forever, reaching what is termed a 'cold death', as the energy of the stars is used up and only barren rock and dust remains.

some kind of super-God (perhaps we can call them Godparents)? Or in order to avoid an infinite regress of explanations, can we suggest that God caused himself? Alternatively, can we simply assert that God has no cause, and leave it at that? God would just be a 'brute fact' – a fact that cannot be explained or needs no explanation. But is that helpful? Would it not be just as reasonable to assert that the universe itself just *is*, and needs no explanation?

A further objection might be to ask 'What is the problem with an infinite sequence of natural causes?' The concern here is that although the meaning of infinity is clear as a concept, an actual infinity is impossible, and in particular an infinite amount of past time is impossible. The argument runs as follows: Before the present event could occur, the event immediately before it would have to occur; and before that event could occur, the event immediately before *that* would have to occur; and so on *ad infinitum*. In this way, causation gets driven back into the past, making it impossible for any event to have occurred. Thus, if the series of events were beginningless, the present could not have occurred, which is absurd. If we don't have a beginning, we don't have a starting point for our chain of causally related events – a point to press 'play' and watch the universe develop. However, not everyone finds this argument convincing, as it relies on the idea that you have to go back for an infinite amount of time to get to the beginning of the chain of events. We can see that this is not so by considering the fact that we can fit an infinite number of points on a line of a finite length. If the line represents the passage of time and each point represents an event, then we can see that we only need go back a finite amount of time to get to the start of an infinite sequence of events.

We might wonder if it is even reasonable to ask whether the universe had an ultimate first cause. To paraphrase Terry Pratchett, in the beginning there was nothing. Then it exploded. Perhaps the popular conception of the Big Bang is that in the beginning there was just empty space. Then, an amount of matter came into existence *ex nihilo* and exploded. However this is not the way that physicists see it. Rather, the 'nothing' was not just the absence of matter, but the absence of space and time as well. The Big Bang marks the point before which there was no space, time or matter, at least, not in *our* universe. And therefore it may not even make sense to talk about *before* the Big Bang, because the word 'before' means 'temporally prior to', but at that point there may not have been any time in which the prior events could take place. This would prevent the Big Bang from being caused, as there was no time in which this preliminary causation event could have taken place. Now this might not seem to be a problem for the proponent of the Cosmological Argument, who may claim that God, with his infinite power, can operate outside time and space. But we might reasonably ask if this claim is meaningful. Can God operate outside time and space when interacting with something that is spatial and temporal, like the universe? What does 'outside' space even mean? In this context, is a claim that God created the universe really saying anything more than "we don't really understand how it all came about"?

Finally, the idea that certain events *cause* other events might be how we understand the world to work, but do we have any grounds to believe that this really is the way the world operates? As David Hume pointed out in the 18th century, all we actually ever see is one event taking place after another[vi]. Our most successful scientific theories show objects appearing to obey certain laws of nature, and in that sense it appears reasonable to say that the current state of affairs was *caused* by the preceding state of affairs. And yet in the 20th Century, the development of quantum physics explained certain events at the sub-atomic level as spontaneous and so 'uncaused'. For example, in respect of phenomena such as radioactive decay, our theories can tell us the likelihood of decay occurring in a particular timeframe, but the exact time at which the event actually occurs appears to be unpredictable. The event occurs spontaneously, rather than as a direct consequence of the events that precede it. Might such phenomena provide evidence that our human tendency to look for causes in every situation could be misguided?

The Ontological Argument

The third classical argument for the existence of God, and the last one I will consider here, is known as the Ontological Argument. It was thought up by the Benedictine monk, Saint Anselm of Cantebury, who lived from 1033 to 1109 and proceeds as follows:-

God is a perfect being
It is better to exist than not to exist
Therefore God exists

At face value, this argument might appear to make sense. Given that it is better to exist than not exist and that God has all the best properties, then God must exist. Yet something feels wrong. Perhaps it is that the argument feels somewhat circular. God, as a concept, may be defined as an entity with all the best properties, but that is just the definition of a concept. Whether this concept refers to anything in the real world, is a separate question. This is the criticism most famously made by German philosopher Immanuel Kant (1724-1804), when he argued that existence is not a predicate – a predicate being a property that an object may have, for example, that of being all-powerful. Consider a similar argument that proceeds as follows:-

God is a perfect being
It is better to be all-powerful than not
Therefore God is all-powerful

This argument feels better – but note that it can be taken in two ways, based on how we interpret the first statement that God is a perfect being. If this is just taken as defining the concept of God, then the argument looks to show that being 'all-powerful' is included in the concept of God (because perfection is having the all the best properties and being all-powerful is one of the best properties to have). Note that under this line of reasoning we are purely discussing abstract concepts; we have not considered whether these concepts refer to anything real. On the other hand, we could take the first statement, that God is a perfect being, as not discussing a concept, but instead describing God, the real entity. This would then indeed show that God, the real entity, is all-powerful, but the problem now is that the approach assumes at the start that God is a real entity. Let's now move back to the first argument – the one that tries to show that God exists. If we are discussing God as an abstract concept, then perhaps it might be claimed to show that the concept of God includes the concept of existing, but it still doesn't show that these things we are discussing are anything more than abstract concepts. On the other hand, if we are discussing God as a real entity, then we have assumed at the start that God exists, which is the very thing we are trying to prove. This is known in logical parlance as 'begging the question'.

Finally, it has been argued that if God is all-powerful, then if he didn't exist, he could will himself into existence. But hold on a minute – if he didn't exist, then surely he wouldn't be in a position to make the choice about whether to exist or not. Can one argue that an all-powerful being could will itself into existence? After all, if the being could not do this, then we are placing a limit on its power, whereas we have already said that it is all-powerful?! Philosophers have come up with limits to God's power before by asking if he can do the logically impossible. For example, one can ask whether God can create something that is too heavy for him to lift. If he can, then his power of lifting is limited. If he can't, then his power of creativity is limited.

Present Day Arguments

The three classic arguments for the existence of God have been subject to strong challenge over the centuries and it might be said that this has put theists on the defensive. 'Reformed Epistemology' is a bullish attempt to get on the front foot, by changing the nature of the debate. The approach emerged from the Reformed Christian tradition in the United States – it is the Christianity that is reformed, rather than the epistemology.

The argument starts from the point of view of our individuals in the Introduction who experience God directly and therefore have no doubts. We said that these lucky few may experience God as immediately as you or I experience the sun and the sky. Or perhaps a tree. But nitpickers are then tempted to ask if we can be sure that it really is a tree that we are experiencing[2] and not perhaps just the illusion of a tree or a mirage. Particularly if it is a palm tree in the desert. And so one might ask if those who experience God directly really are experiencing God, or might they perhaps just be deluding themselves? To get around this, Reformed Epistemologists would equate experiencing God with say, seeing something green. We cannot doubt that we are seeing something green – whether it is a mirage or a real tree, it is still green. The experience of a green patch is therefore what philosophers call 'basic'. In establishing our knowledge, we start with what is basic and cannot be doubted, and work our way up from there. Reformed Epistemologists argue that because experience of God is basic, there is no need to justify it; indeed it *cannot* be justified in other more basic terms.

We will be in a better position to understand whether this argument stands up to scrutiny later on, but for now, one point stands out and that is that this argument is not persuasive to those who don't already believe in God. You can substitute anything you like into this argument in place of the Christian God and it will have the same logical force. We could use this form of argument to claim that Zeus exists or why not the giant invisible ghost unicorns that stride majestically through the cosmos? Now while Reformed Epistemologists would accept that these parallel arguments do indeed have the same logical force, for them, this is a side issue. Their main point is that because they experience God directly, they know that if you disagree that the Christian God exists, then you are wrong. And they know that if you claim that giant invisible ghost unicorns exist then you are *taking the Micky*. The Reformed Epistemologist says more than just "you can't prove that I'm wrong to claim that God exists". They also say "If you can't see that God exists, then you need to open yourself up. You are wrong and wilfully in denial." We reach an impasse.

In the latter part of the twentieth century, an alternative position on the existence of God was developed, known as Anti-Realism[vii] or Religious Minimalism. This position developed out of considerations regarding what is meant by asserting that a given statement is true. This can be a

[2] It is common in philosophical discussion to use 'experiencing' to mean seeing, hearing, smelling, touching etc.

complex subject and I will leave detailed discussion until Chapter 12. But perhaps the common sense understanding of truth is that a statement is true if its assertion corresponds to the actual facts of the situation. So, for example, the statement 'the night sky is black' is true, because we know the meaning of 'night sky' and 'black' and so it is a fact that the night sky is indeed black, rather than white, for example. Philosophers call this the 'Correspondence theory of truth'.

An alternative conception is that a statement is true if it is accepted as true within a community and is consistent with the other beliefs and assertions within that community. So for example, the statements 'God exists' and 'Mary was a virgin' are true, if accepted as true within the community. Now on the face of it, this may look like a licence to close your eyes, put your fingers in your ears, disregard what is happening in the world and believe what you like, but the position is more subtle than that. For a statement to be considered true, it must cohere with other statements accepted as true within the community. So if the inside of a windowless room with the lights off appears black, it would not 'cohere' with a claim that the night sky is white. This approach is known as the 'Coherence Theory of Truth'[viii].

Critics of anti-realism point to the verificationist underpinnings of this position[ix]. We recognise that it can't be claimed that the night sky is white, because we can verify that this is not so, by looking at the evidence. However, for a claim like 'Mary was a virgin', we do not have sufficient evidence to be able to confirm it. The anti-realist says this gives us a licence to be able to insist that it is true, at least within the anti-realist community. Critics argue that it is more appropriate to treat it as an unverifiable hypothesis.

A closely related idea is that of Fictionalism. This is less concerned with whether religious statements are true, in the sense of corresponding to objective facts about the world, and more interested in providing a beneficial framework to live by[x]. The contemporary philosopher of religion Don Cupitt said that he is a Christian priest because he lives by the fiction of the Christian story. We are invited to suspend disbelief and enter into this other world of alternative facts. On this picture, the different religious claims of different communities are not *disputing* what others consider to be facts; they are instead offering different frameworks to live by.

The question is then raised as to whether Fictionalists or Anti-realists have any views about whether God really exists outside the context of the community belief framework. Under the Coherence theory of truth, there is no claim that the concept of God corresponds to any actual being, in the traditional sense of a creator who is apart from the world and sustains it. It is perhaps more helpful to think of God like we think of the equator – it does not exist in a physical sense, but it exists as a concept to help us make sense of the world. This is all very well, but it can surely now be objected that anti-realists are using the word 'God' differently to how it is normally used. God may well be useful as a concept, but we have not addressed the issue as to whether God exists, in his more usual sense of being a metaphysical entity – a real thing, not just an idea or a concept. Anti-realists such as D. Z. Phillips, an influential philosopher of religion, dismiss this objection, claiming that 'metaphysics is the product of deep confusions about the logic of our language'[xi]. On this view, it doesn't even make sense to ask the question of whether God exists as a real metaphysical being, and so it is only the role God plays in our culture that counts. However his position has been challenged by critics such as J. L. Mackie who essentially argue that if it is accepted that God doesn't exist as a real metaphysical object, then he can only exist in a metaphorical sense, which is to say he doesn't really exist at all!

Things get complicated very quickly, so we will leave at that for now. We will be in a better position to assess the force of these arguments towards the end of this book.

So to recap, we have now covered the most famous arguments for the existence of God, and if any of these arguments persuade you that God exists, then the question is resolved for you and there is no need to read on. If, on the other hand, you find these arguments unconvincing, then the question remains unresolved and we need to consider other approaches to try to settle it one way or the other. And given that science has been so successful in extending our knowledge of the world around us, perhaps adopting a more scientific approach to the question of whether God exist will help us make more progress.

Chapter 3

3. Solving Mysteries the Modern Way

The Atheist view might imply that the way the world operates can, in principle, be understood without the need to refer to any supernatural being. But perhaps this is a point that is in need of closer examination. Is it reasonable to believe that God and science are incompatible, or at least that science makes God redundant? After all, there have been many famous and brilliant scientists who were religious, for example Isaac Newton. Although more recent research has suggested that his religious views were unorthodox, perhaps as one might expect of a learned physicist in a more conservative time, he was nevertheless a believer[xii]. Albert Einstein on the other hand, does not fit neatly into either the theistic or atheist camp, having famously stated that "Science without religion is lame, religion without science is blind"[xiii]. For this reason, the first step in our enquiry is to take a closer look at exactly what science does, and perhaps more importantly what it does not, tell us about the world around us.

Modern theories of physics describe the interactions between the fundamental particles of nature and this in turn allows us to understand the behaviour and interactions of atoms and molecules. An understanding of molecular behaviour allows us to understand proteins and amino acids, which in turn leads us to understand the behaviour of cells. The behaviour of cells allows us to understand the operation of the organs of the body and so, at least in principle, we are in a position to understand ourselves. Physics explains chemistry and chemistry explains biology, as is often said. Where then, is there room for God in all of this? Do we need God built into our scientific theories in order to accept him as consistent with a science based picture of the universe?

Atheists who smile triumphantly at the staggering force of this argument might do well to note that a similar kind of question can be asked about free will. Where does free will fit in to this mechanistic universe of ours, which runs with particles interacting with each other like clockwork? For example, you might believe that you have chosen to read this paragraph about free will, and could have equally chosen to do something else instead. But could you have? Given that the movement of your limbs is determined by electrical signals from your brain, and that these signals are a result of chemical and electrical processes within the brain, all of which obey the laws of nature, then did you really have any choice? It may only *appear* to you that you decided to read this paragraph, and that in reality your body was just obeying the laws of nature and there was never a possibility of any other outcome. Against this, some may argue that there is genuine free will if there is a separate non-physical soul. Or perhaps that the randomness characteristic of quantum mechanics at the sub-atomic level presents us with an opportunity to argue that our 'choices' are not determined in advance.

Another avenue for consideration is the idea that, rather than our current level of scientific understanding being incomplete – since we have no fundamental theory to cover God and the soul – the explanation is more that these concepts apply at a different level. We might note that although at the physical objective level, the universe may play out like clockwork, at the human level, we do make choices about what we are going to do next. In the same way, it could be argued that a materialistic picture of the universe does not rule out the possibility of God and the impact of prayer; it is just a description on a different level. Perhaps at the level of human thought you are praying and it is having an effect. But at the level of atoms, it is just forces and particles interacting. However in order for this idea to be accepted as more than just wishful thinking, we would need to see the development of a credible model showing how the operations at each level correspond. When you pray and God listens, what is happening at the physical level?

In any event, given the remarkable success of the scientific method over the centuries in extending our knowledge about the world, might it be possible to design an experiment to detect God, or at least to detect God's influence on the world? In April 2006, the American Heart Journal reported on the results of the largest study yet undertaken into the effect of intercessory prayer on the recovery of patients who had undergone cardiac bypass surgery[xiv]. The study was designed using randomised, blind trials, and involved more than 1,800 patients. Prayer groups were asked to pray for a successful surgery and a quick, healthy recovery and no complications. Could the force of prayer make a difference? In that case, the results showed that the prayers had no beneficial effect on patients' recovery 30 days after surgery. What can we infer from such studies about the power of prayer?

We might imagine an experiment, for example, where a group of believers are asked to pray that the outcome of the roll of a dice will yield a six. One might expect that a sympathetic and good God will respond to prayer and therefore, if this experiment were to be repeated many times, we would find that a six has been obtained more than one sixth of the time, or perhaps more than was obtained in a parallel trial undertaken by a control group who did not pray for a certain outcome. We might note that the Bible says in Proverbs 16:33, "We may throw the dice, but the Lord determines how they fall"!

So let's say the experiment is run. How do we interpret the results? Of course, we immediately run into problems. Suppose the die is rolled 6,000 times and we get 1,050 sixes. Does this prove that God exists or could this have happened by chance? Statisticians and people who have studied A Level maths can tell you that the probability of getting 1,050 or more sixes by chance is around 5% or 1 in 20. Does this prove that God exists? As we are talking about probabilities, it is not black and white. For some, a 1 in 20 event actually occurring is pretty unlikely. You wouldn't bet your house on a 1 in 20 event and so this may be good evidence that God does exist. For others there is room for reasonable doubt. A 1 in 20 event is much more likely than, say, a 1 in a million event, which most might agree would be pretty conclusive. This experimental outcome might be said to provide evidence, but not *proof* that God exists.

How about looking at it the other way? Does this not prove that God does *not* exist? Would we not expect a lot more sixes if a large number of his fervent believers were using the full force of prayer to influence the outcome? Does the fact that the outcome is not significantly different from that obtained by pure chance not illustrate that either a) God does not have the power to influence the world in the way that an almighty being might be expected to or b) he does not respond to his believers? This latter explanation is the view taken by Epicurus (341–270 BC) and his followers. They claimed that the gods are 'thin' – that they may exist, but they take no interest in influencing the human world. Events can be explained in naturalistic terms. Of course, if God does exist, it could easily be argued that God is not a machine that automatically responds to all prayers. God exercises discretion and only responds to those prayers that are deemed worthy. And who can know the mind of God? Even if a cause appears worthy to us, perhaps God is acting with a bigger picture in mind. God might not therefore be expected to stoop to the level of indulging humanity in these games. And indeed arguably therefore, knowing this, true believers may not have prayed for a six with the same fervour that that they would apply when praying for the good health of a loved one, for example. It could be argued that were God to reveal himself, incontrovertibly to humanity, then something would be lost. 'Faith' or 'Belief' in God would no longer be required if his existence were an established fact. But is not faith a virtue that is to be lauded? I have faith that my loved ones will be there for me when I am in trouble and I would be hurt if they did not believe I would be there for them. Likewise, I have faith that my lover is not cheating on me and I don't need to put her under surveillance in order to establish this beyond all reasonable doubt, because I don't have doubt. Attempting to directly 'prove' the existence of God implies, it might be argued, that you don't consider God worthy of your faith. And what can be more worthy of faith than a being that is the ultimate good? Framing the issue this way might suggest that the problem is with the unbeliever, who needs to more carefully consider their own values!

What if the prayer group observed 3,000 sixes from the 6,000 rolls? Or 6,000 sixes? The probabilities of these results happening by chance are so miniscule that almost nobody would believe that this was just a freak result that did indeed occur by chance. This would surely be proof beyond all reasonable doubt that God existed. Perhaps believers would view this as a miracle! However, it is perhaps more likely that most would view such a result with an element of suspicion. As alluded to above, many might view it as highly unusual of God, if he exists, to respond to prayer in such an overt manner. Might it be instead, that the experiment was fixed – that actually the die was weighted, or loaded in such a way as to make a six outcome more likely? Perhaps these results were a pure fabrication? Even if the event was filmed, could camera tricks have been used to convey a false picture of what actually occurred?

Having said that, from time to time, experiments or observations do come along that force us to rethink everything we think we know about how the world works, and we shall look at some examples of this in Chapter 5. However it seems that however conclusive the experiment, there are always those sceptics who refuse to accept the new paradigm. It seems that ultimately, whatever the outcome of an experiment, there is always more than one way of interpreting the result, and so experiments such as the dice rolling one discussed above cannot provide conclusive proof of the existence of God one way or the other. And so a lot people take this to mean that humanity can never establish beyond all doubt whether or not God exists. You just have to believe what you believe and in the final reckoning, you will find out if you were right[3]. If God exists. If he doesn't, then when you die you will go to oblivion and won't find out anything at all.

[3] Or will you? We will discuss this further later.

The 17th Century French mathematician Blaise Pascal used this logic to make the point that it is much safer to believe in God than not. Essentially, if God exists, then if you believe in him, you rise to heaven when you die. If you didn't believe in him, then you are castigated in the fiery pits of Hell as an unbeliever. On the other hand, if he doesn't exist, then you enter oblivion either way and have lost nothing! This is known as 'Pascal's Wager'.

One objection to the way this is framed may be whether God would really damn you for eternity as an unbeliever if you had otherwise led a good and virtuous life. But perhaps the principle objection has to be whether you can simply *choose* to believe in God if you want to. Can you just decide to believe that the sky is green? Even if, supposing you were an atheist, you went to great lengths to convince yourself that God exists, by going to regular worship and immersing yourself in the religious culture, it is unlikely that you would be able to remove all doubt.

So we are back to the thought that it is impossible determine with certainty, irrespective of the evidence that could be presented to us, whether or not God exists. Is this conclusion inescapable?

Chapter 4

4. Being Human and the Limits of Knowledge

In order to answer the question of whether God exists, i.e. of whether there is a God as part of this amazing reality that we inhabit, we need to understand something of the nature of this reality. Part of the reason why the question of whether God exists has proved so problematic up to now, is due to our pre-conceived notions or 'commonsense' beliefs regarding what this reality is like. We considered in chapter one how the apparently reasonable commonsense beliefs underpinning the scientific realist worldview lead to a dead end in answering the question of whether or not God exists, but noted that these underpinnings could be challenged. And so the purpose of the next part of this book is to consider the grounds for some of these commonsense underpinnings. I will argue that this results in a better way of understanding what reality is like, which will in turn give us what we need to flesh out our answer to the question of whether or not God exists. Albert Einstein once remarked that common sense consists of all the prejudices one learns before the age of eighteen, a comment that suggests we really ought to examine some of these early-imbibed notions in detail.

If we accept the story told by common sense, reality consists of space, an invisible substrate which extends out indefinitely in all directions, and time, which flows uniformly on. Set in this reality are a number of interacting objects, which make up the world around us. As individuals, we are born into this world, as a further object. When our eyes are opened and our cognitive functions are in working order, the world floods in and knowledge of it results. God, if he exists, is considered as another of these objects, although perhaps not a physical object. Conventional religious doctrine also includes concepts such as the soul, Heaven and Hell – how do they fit into the commonsense picture? While they can no longer be thought of as 'above' and 'below' the world for the space-age consciousness, this is not necessarily a problem. For example, they could be conceived of as 'parallel' spaces, to which we only have access when we die.

Under this commonsense picture of reality, the question of whether God exists is undecidable. We have already explored a number of different experiments designed to establish whether or not God exists and they all ended in failure. The problem is that in the end, we only experience God's presence indirectly, if at all, so who is to say whether the cause of any such event is God or something else? Even were the clouds to part and God to reveal himself in all his glory, could we be sure afterwards that this was not a dream or a hallucination?

Our current 'commonsense' picture of reality has been built up over time, but is heavily influenced by the reality described by Newton's laws of motion that we learn about at school. These classical laws proved so successful, that they shaped the thought of society through the Enlightenment period and beyond. Newton is often considered the 'father' of the Enlightenment. However, more recently, the theories of relativity and quantum mechanics have superseded Newton's theories and proved themselves to be more successful, particularly in describing the world of the very large and the very small. And yet these more modern descriptions of reality produce more or less the same results as classical theories at the everyday, commonsense level and so are rarely taught to the general public at school. It is perhaps for this reason that the challenges they bring to our view of reality scarcely enter the public consciousness. When they do, they may be seen as little more than interesting curiosities which have no real importance for our everyday lives. For us, however, the next step is to look more closely at the world of the very large and the very small and see how that challenges our conventional view of how the world operates.

One might imagine that if you look though a microscope or a telescope, you will see the world behaving in a similar way to how we experience it every day, just at a different scale. So when we think of an atom, we think of electrons orbiting the nucleus in the same way that planets go around the sun. While alive to the idea that things might be different at these vast and miniscule scales, our expectations will be based on what we are already familiar with, because what else can they be based on?

Let's consider the world of the miniscule first. With a microscope, you can see what micro-organisms like bacteria look like. Bacteria are approximately 1 micron (μm) or 1000th of a millimetre in size, which is around the limit of what can be seen with optical microscopy. This is because the visible light used in optical microscopy has a wavelength of slightly below 1 micron. It follows that in order to achieve a higher resolution, you need a microscope that uses particles with a shorter wavelength, such as electrons. A transmission electron microscope works by firing electrons, rather than shining visible light, through the specimen being observed. And because our eyes are not capable of detecting electrons, the resultant image is projected onto a screen or a photographic plate. The contrast within the image results from the specimen scattering electrons by different amounts in different areas, just like how an optical microscope magnifies scattered light. Electron microscopes can reach resolutions of less than one Angstrom (Å) which is one ten thousandth of a micron (10^{-10}m). This is small enough to see individual atoms!

Traditional electron microscopes suffer from blurring, caused by technological limitations which mean the electron beam cannot be focused precisely on the detector. However, more recent images of atoms are composed using sophisticated 3D reconstruction algorithms to remove the blurring by comparing a number of different blurred images. Any remaining blurring that can be seen is then principally a result of the vibration of the atoms themselves.

It perhaps seems incredible that technology has reached the stage where we can see individual atoms! But at this point someone might legitimately ask whether we can really be said to be 'seeing' the atoms. With the optical microscope, you look through a lens and see the bacteria as they would naturally appear to you if you had better eyesight. Yes, the fact that we are looking through a lens changes what we see, but there is a lens at the front of each of our eyes which focuses incoming light onto the retina – so this changes what we see too.

If we are short-sighted or long-sighted, we see the world differently to someone with 20/20 vision, due to the lens at the front of our eye not focusing the light properly onto the retina. We correct our blurred vision with glasses or contact lenses, so that we can see the world 'properly'. The situation with an electron microscope is different. What are we actually looking at? In the first instance, we are looking at a piece of paper or a screen. The image on this piece of paper/screen is generated by electrons that are scattered by the object we are examining. So in that sense we are seeing a representation of the atoms, rather than seeing the atoms as they really are.

This, of course, is analogous to looking at a standard photograph. In this case, we are looking at a picture of an object, rather than the object itself. If I were to position my eyes close to the picture, would it appear just the same as if I was looking at the actual object in the picture? There are differences – how pronounced these are will depend on the camera. Colours may be different – some cameras cope better with shades of red, at the end of the visible spectrum, than others. Of course, black and white photographs will have no colour at all. There is also the issue of depth of field – some cameras will have almost the whole shot in focus. When you look at something in real life, it is only the very centre of your vision that is in focus. To convince yourself of this, consider how you read a book. Can you do this by staring at one fixed spot, or do you need to sweep your gaze back and forth across the page? Try focusing on the 'XYZ' in the sequence of letters below and at the same time, trying to read some of the outer letters!

pqasfsdafsdafsdafsdafXYZaefsdfasdfasdfsdafsdpq

So there are differences between the images generated by our cameras and microscopes and the images that are produced in our mind's eye, when looking at an object directly. The images generated by our microcscopes can be said to be representations of the objects we are wanting to observe, but we are not seeing them as they 'really are'. Consider a photograph of atoms for example. The photograph shows us the structure of the atoms within the crystal, but what about the colours? The image is produced by electrons, whereas colour is a property of visible light. In images produced by electron microscopes, colour is added afterwards rather than resulting from the object being examined.

We might therefore conclude that electron microscopes and other technology can give us representations of objects, that provide more information about them, but they do not show these objects as they really are. This means that in order to interpret these images, we need to be mindful of the relationship between the image and the object that it is representing. For example, when we look at old black and white photographs, of course we do not think that there was no colour in the world at that time. We are conscious that this is a result of the technology – that only some of the information has been captured in the image. But what if we don't know any better? When the first colour photograph of the surface of Mars taken from the Viking 1 lander in July 1976 was released, it showed a blue sky. However, it was soon realised that the colour had not been calibrated correctly and an updated photograph was released a few days later showing the red sky that we are all familiar with today. To avoid being misled by such images, we need not only the information in the image, but also the context. We need to understand how to interpret the information given to us.

Now what about when we look at objects directly? Are we seeing things as they really are, or again, is it only some of the information that is being captured? I see the laptop in front of me right now and I imagine you can see the book or ereader in front of you, right now. It is clear to us that it exists. If I now turn around and look behind me, I can no longer see the laptop. Does it still exist? This was a question considered by Irish clergyman come philosopher Bishop George Berkeley (1685-1753) who offered philosophy the astonishing principle *Esse est Percipi* or 'To be is to be perceived'[xv]. Berkeley argued that we have no grounds to believe that objects exist if we are not perceiving them. At face value at least, this claim does seem remarkable, given that I can confirm that the laptop still exists, just by turning my head back around. However, the claim might be said to receive some support from the Copenhagen interpretation of quantum mechanics, as we will see later. Berkeley's way out of this hole that he had dug for himself was to answer that for an object to exist, it need only be the case that *someone* is perceiving it – that someone doesn't have to be you. And handily for Berkeley, God is a someone who can perceive everything everywhere all at once. This idea is summed up in a subsequent limerick about a tree in the quad:-

There was a young man who said "God
must think it exceedingly odd
if he finds that this tree
Continues to be
when no-one's about in the Quad"

and the reply

Dear sir, your astonishment's odd
I am always about in the Quad
And that's why this tree
continues to be
Since observed by yours faithfully, God

Interestingly, it comes as no surprise to me when I turn back around to find that the laptop is still there. We don't need our parents to say, 'Don't worry – based on innumerable tests, physicists have it on good authority that there is an external world that continues to exist, even when you are not looking at it. Phew! On the contrary, it seems to be hardwired into our subconscious that the object is just there, so when it is in our field of view, we can see it.

But back to the scientific view of reality. Developments in neuroscience in recent decades reveal that the human body gathers sense data with c. 200 million sensory receptor cells, fewer than 3 million sensory fibres and 16 billion cortical cells. Unfortunately, the brain doesn't have the storage capacity or energy to process all this information[xvi]. This discovery has interesting implications. Our basic understanding of how we view the world under the common-sense picture outlined above is that if our cognitive functions are in working order, information about the world floods in and knowledge of the world results. But this discovery shows that our knowledge of the world is necessarily limited. Even if our sensory organs were capable of detecting everything about the world, we are simply not big-brained enough to be able to process all this information and provide a comprehensive picture of it to our conscious mind.

The brain therefore discards most of the information it receives. This is an unconscious, yet active process. This can be illustrated by the famous optical illusion known as Troxler's Fading.

Troxler's fading

If you focus on the dot at the centre for long enough, you will notice parts of the outer ring disappear. The brain is discarding the information that it views as less important. So here is an example you can see for yourself where the object is in front of us, but there are times when we don't see it. Not because it is invisible to humans in the sense that the eye cannot perceive the light frequencies involved, but because the brain chooses to disregard it. This is a crucial point. Most of us might think that our sense organs are like a passive filter. Some sounds we can hear and some we cannot. Some frequencies of light we can see, like the visible spectrum and some we cannot, like the infra-red and ultraviolet. But we might think that reality as presented to us by our brains will reflect the information received by our senses. Experiments such as Troxler's fading show that this is not so. Our brains play an *active* role in determining what reality looks like to us.

Modern neuroscience is of the view that rather than merely discard information that is not deemed useful, the brain will on occasion actively present us with a made up picture of the world[xvii]. Perhaps the most famous example where this might apply is in the blind spot. The retina at the back of your eyeball is covered with around 130 million photoreceptors which transform incoming light into signals sent to the brain. The nerve fibres from each photoreceptor come together in a bundle called the optic nerve at the back of the eyeball. Here, there are no photoreceptors, so incoming light striking this part of the retina will not be detected. The blind spot is quite large – if you hold an orange up in front of you and move it into the blind spot, you can make it disappear! To try this, start by covering your left eye and hold an orange up in front of you with your right hand. Look with your right eye, not at the orange, but at a reference point directly in front of you and maintain your focus on that. Now start with the orange in line with the reference point and then slowly bring it to the right, and very slightly below your line of sight. When the orange is about 15 cm away from your line of sight, you will notice in your peripheral vision that parts of the orange start disappearing. You can then manoeuvre it so that the whole orange is no longer visible. What is going on here? The orange is within your overall field of vision but cannot be detected by your eye. How does the brain deal with this?

We spoke above about the differences between the image in a photo and the image created by your mind's eye. It is perhaps natural to think of consciousness as a 'little person' that sits in your head, a bit like a pilot in control of a giant robot. This pilot monitors the screens that display all the data received from the eyes and other senses and then directs the robot's movements. At first sight, you might expect the blind spot to be perceived as a fuzzy piece of white noise in your field of vision. But that wouldn't make sense. If each photoreceptor on your eyeball mapped to a pixel on a video display for example, then any gap between the photoreceptors doesn't mean there needs to be a corresponding gap on the display. But instead we might expect to see a distorted picture on the display, due to the fact that the gridlike layout of the pixels is not able to replicate the layout of the photoreceptors. But this doesn't seem to be the case either. When the orange disappears into the blind spot, we don't notice any kind of distortion, with straight lines bending to get around the gap.

One way to get around this problem, is to hypothesise that the brain makes something up. A best guess as to what would make sense to be there. It can be noted that when a pencil is moved such that the tip is in the blind spot, the tip disappears from view. However, if the pencil is raised such that it passes through the blind spot, with the base below and the tip above, we don't see a gap in the middle of the pencil. Under this 'filling in' hypothesis, the brain is completing the picture with a 'made-up' bit of pencil filling in the gap where the real pencil cannot be detected.

However, there is an alternative view that this is the wrong way of looking at it, explored by thinkers such as Daniel Dennett (Consciousness Explained 1992) and J. Kevin O'Regan, (Why Red Doesn't Sound Like a Bell 2011). The alternative views holds that the idea of a 'TV screen in our minds' is not right. The TV screen concept immediately raises the question "Who is looking at the TV screen?" If the answer is that it is this 'little person', we can ask how this little person transforms the TV image into the image that we actually see. If the answer is that the TV image *is* the image that we see, then we can ask what is wrong with saying that the information being taken from the photoreceptors in the eye is the image that we see?

Now there are many more photoreceptors at the centre of our retina than around the edges. If we get rid of this internal TV screen idea, then we would expect the image that we see to be sharper in the middle and blurry around the edges. And this is indeed in line with what we already noted above. So why is it that we are not generally conscious of the world as blurry in the main?

The answer, on this alternative view, is that our perspective on the world is not primarily based on what is being received by our senses at a given point in time. Rather, our perspective is based on the brain's understanding of the world – the sense data is merely used to confirm or modify this understanding. The idea that the brain produces a model of the universe dates back to 19th Century German physiologist and polymath Herman van Helmholtz. My brain understands that the laptop is still there when I turn away. In the same way, our understanding knows that the letters in our peripheral vision are not really blurry – this can be confirmed at any time, by focussing our vision on the letters in question. When we hold the pencil across our blind spot, it is blurry due to the fewer photoreceptors involved in that part of our field of vision. The reason there is no gap in the image of the pencil that we see, is purely down to the fact that there is no gap in the pencil itself! When we focus our gaze back on the pencil, we see it in its full detail, as expected.

However, it may also be noted that the active modelling that the brain does can lead to a *false* understanding of the way the world is. An example that many of us will be familiar with at the moment is phantom vibration syndrome. Many of us keep our mobile phones in our pockets and the phone vibrates to alert us to new notifications. How many of us have felt that vibration, only to find that no new notification has been received? Was the vibration real or just imagined? This example shows how, like hallucinations, information we think we are receiving about the world does not always have an external source and is just part of the brain's model of the real world. And this model is sometimes misleading. For another interesting example, we can consider the 'rubber hand experiment'. This is a classic you can watch on the internet or, even better, do at home with a partner. One person acts as a guinea pig and sits with one forearm resting on the table in front of them. There is also a rubber forearm with a rubber hand on the end of it on the table. The forearm is positioned so that, to the guinea pig, it looks like it could be their own arm – a cloth is generally used to cover their real arm. Sometimes a box or a screen is used, but the key point is that the arm and the rubber arm are positioned such that only the rubber hand is visible to the guinea pig. The experimenter sits opposite and has sight of both the guinea pig's hand and the rubber hand.

The experimenter uses two brushes to simultaneously stroke the knuckles of the guinea pig's hand (all out of sight of the guinea pig) and the rubber hand (which the guinea pig can see). After about a minute, the guinea pig begins to feel that the rubber hand is 'their' hand! What is going on here? The brain is reconciling the stimulus it is getting from the eyes with the stimulus it is getting from the skin. Once again, the brain is building an understanding of the world which reconciles with the incoming sense data.

This again supports the idea that the brain is giving you a picture of the universe that is consistent with the incoming data signals, rather than showing you what is actually 'out there'. In the film, 'The Matrix', people spend their lives arrayed in pods of fluid, with a stimulus cable plugged directly into their heads. This cable supplies information directly to the nerve fibres, bypassing the receptors in each individual's sensory organs. The brain conjures up a reality that is consistent with the incoming data signals from the Matrix, namely city life in the year 1999.

And of course, the way the world appears to me, may not be the same as the way it appears to you. For example, researchers have established that dogs do not see the full range of colours that we do, and generally experience the world in shades of grey, yellow and blue. Research also indicates that dogs see the things at a distance as blurrier than we do.

Human view Dog view

The images above show how an aeroplane appears to us in contrast with how we would expect a dog to see it. Who is seeing the plane as it really is? The answer is of course, 'neither'. Both the human and dog are seeing the plane as represented to them by their brains, based on the incoming data signals from our optical apparatus. So what does the real plane look like? Of course, it makes no sense to ask what the 'real' plane looks like – for the plane to look like anything, there needs to be someone doing the looking.

Instead, we can try to go beyond how it *appears* and ask how it *is*. Our aim here is to remove the subjectivity of the observer. So what is an aeroplane? It is big and made of metal. And what is metal? It is a hard and shiny substance. That is the way metal *appears* to our sense of touch and our sense of vision. Tell me what it is aside from how it appears. In his book 'An Essay Concerning Human Understanding', the English philosopher John Locke (1632-1704)[xviii] divided the properties of objects into what he called Primary and Secondary qualities. Primary qualities are those intrinsic to an object itself, and Locke gives examples such as size, shape and speed. Secondary qualities are those that are determined by the object's relationship to the observer. So the colour of the aeroplane is a secondary quality, because it has a different colour from the dog's perspective than it has from the human perspective. We can go beyond how the plane appears though, when we consider its size, which according to Locke is independent of the observer and so an intrinsic property of the object.

If as theories go, this appears reasonable, it also raises the question of how we decide whether such and such a property is a Primary or Secondary quality. Can we be sure, for example, that the size of an object is intrinsic to the object as it is in itself or could it be that it may be different for different observers, as implied by Einstein's relativity theory? This is crucial if we are going to understand whether it makes sense to ask whether God *actually* exists, rather than just *appearing* to exist and I will return to this question in some detail later.

To explore further how to see the world as it really is, we need to think about how knowledge about the universe around us is acquired and what the limits of this are. This is a branch of philosophy called epistemology. Historically, humanity has used a number of different methods of finding out more about the universe. In societies past, people have consulted soothsayers, seers and other such mystics who have appeared to have access to hidden knowledge. But how do we know if their prophesies are reliable?

Our knowledge of the world around us consists of the set of facts, or true statements, about the world. For example 'the sun rises in the east each day' and 'leaves fall off the trees in autumn' may be considered facts about the world. On the other hand 'The earth has several moons' would usually not be considered a true statement. Yet note here the importance of being clear about our definitions. What do we mean by a moon? If a moon means any object orbiting the earth, then the statement that the earth has many moons could be said to be true.

There are other statements that can be made, which would not be considered facts about the world. For example 'the Scottish Highlands is the best place to live'. As this is a matter of opinion, this cannot be considered a fact about the world. Also 'five plus seven equals twelve'. This is a true statement, but it is a true statement within the context of number theory, which is an abstract framework, and is therefore not a fact about the world around us.

Since at least the 17th Century, the most accepted technique used to establish facts about the world is the scientific method. Science might be said to work by trying to figure out how the world must be configured 'behind the scenes' – how it really is – if it is to result in the phenomena that we experience. As we know from school, we start with a hypothesis (an idea) about how the world is configured. We then design an experiment to test whether this idea is correct. A well designed experiment will result in one result (appearance) if the hypothesis is true and a different one if it is false. In this way we can disregard the false hypotheses and only accept the true ones[4]. This approach is appealing because, in theory at least, anyone who doubts whether a hypothesis about the world is true can repeat the experiment and see for themselves. You don't have to rely on taking the word of mystics with supernatural powers.

So where have we got to in our enquiry? What is metal – aside from how it appears? Well in the case of our aeroplane, it is an alloy of titanium and steel. And titanium is a chemical element with atomic number 22, a detail which we can say is a description of what titanium intrinsically is, rather than how it appears. It is through tirelessly amassing and checking such detail that for centuries now, we have used science as the key tool to move beyond the limitations of our senses and uncover what the universe is really like 'behind the scenes' of our everyday perceptions. 20th century physics has revealed that it is actually very different to the way we understand it under the commonsense picture. In the next chapter, we'll take a look at a few of these remarkable discoveries.

[4] See Chapter 7 for more discussion on the Scientific Method

Chapter 5

5. Modern Science and how Common Sense gets it All Wrong

For centuries, science has been furthering our knowledge of how the universe works. At times, these discoveries have been surprising. For example the first proof of a spherical Earth comes from the Greeks in the 5th century BC. And at times they have been astounding – in 1687, Isaac Newton showed how his simple laws of gravitation and motion could describe the behaviour of everything from apples falling from trees to the orbits of planets in the solar system! The 17th Century also saw developments in chemistry with Robert Boyle's ideal gas law and biology with Robert Hooke discovering the cell. By the 19th Century, we have Charles Darwin's theory of evolution, John Dalton's atomic theory, Dmitri Mendeleev's Periodic Table of elements and Gregor Mendel's laws of inheritance, the basis for genetic theory. Developments in the understanding of electricity and magnetism culminated in the classical electromagnetic theory, captured in the four famous equations of James Clerk Maxwell.[xix]

Yet such apparent breakthroughs in science can lead us down the wrong track when it comes to answering the question of whether God exists. It is therefore important to understand how 20th century physics blew a hole in this classical view of the way the universe works.

We are taught the classical view of the universe at school, to such an extent that this picture of the universe seems quite normal, quite *unchallengable*, to us at the beginning of the 21st Century. But it is not difficult to see that many of these discoveries must have been revolutionary when they were made, requiring fundamental changes in how people viewed the universe and their place in it. The orthodox view in the 17th Century, for example, was that the earth was the centre of the universe – promotion of the heliocentric picture was considered heretical by the church. We also know that, for centuries, many in the church viewed the theory of evolution as a threat to a view that placed humanity above other creatures of God's creation. In this context, the march of science might be seen as a lesson in humility; a series of blows to humanity's sense of self-importance, with the universe turning out to be bigger and older and mankind's place in it less central, than was thought previously. And yet, today, there are those who refuse to accept these scientific discoveries and would rather believe in results inferred from religious scripture. There is the 'Creationist' movement that seeks to deny the picture from modern science that the universe is c. 13.8 billion years old and instead believes that the age of the universe is a mere 6,000 or so years; this being a result calculated by Archbishop Ussher in the 17th century from Biblical sources[xx].

However, for those of us who are willing to accept what we are taught at school, our understanding of the universe is likely to be based on the classical picture described above, namely the results of scientific endeavour, more or less up to the end of the 19th Century. This is broadly equivalent to the 'common sense' picture I outlined previously. The universe is seen as an expanse of three-dimensional space in which a multitude of discrete objects are situated. These objects interact with each other by obeying various physical laws, which result in their positions and orientations in space changing with the passage of time.

Now this was all fine at the end of the 19th century. But, as many of us are nowadays vaguely aware, developments in physics in the 20th century have challenged this view – in particular the development of Einstein's theory of Relativity describing the universe at a very large scale and Quantum Mechanics, describing the universe at the very small scale. But, because we are not taught about these developments at school, and most of us have no cause to be dealing with the world on these scales on a regular basis, we don't subject the common-sense picture to serious challenge. The common-sense picture broadly works well, as a way of viewing the universe, so the prevailing strategy is 'if it ain't broke, don't fix it'.

However, as I said at the outset, this common-sense picture misleads us when it comes to exploring the question of whether or not God exists, so let's now spend a few pages outlining some of the most interesting results of 20th century physics, just to give us a flavour of how the common-sense picture of the universe has been undermined.

Six results of 20th Century Physics that appear to defy common sense[xxi]

1. *Nothing can travel faster than light*

Einstein's special theory of relativity states that nothing can travel faster than light[5], and people perhaps accept this as an interesting piece of trivia. But how can that be? What would happen, for example, if I was on a rocket ship travelling at nearly the speed of light, and then someone gave it an extra boost? We would expect the applied force to cause the ship to accelerate and go faster than light, so what is preventing this from happening? Well the only way you can apply a force and the object *not* accelerate is if it has infinite mass! To see this, consider the case when an opportunity arises to overtake the car in front and note how much more slowly your car accelerates when it is loaded with luggage and passengers compared to when it is empty. The heavier the vehicle, the bigger the engine you need to get it to accelerate at the same rate. Now imagine a vehicle so massive (heavy) that no matter how big the engine, it doesn't get any faster when you press the accelerator. This is what relativity says happens to objects as they approach the speed of light. They get more

[5] Or more specifically, no *signal* can travel faster than the speed of light. Some quantum interactions take place instantaneously, but these are random and cannot be used to convey information.

massive and so are unable to breach that threshold. This is new. Under the common-sense picture, an object's mass is an intrinsic property of the object itself and doesn't depend on how fast it is going.

2. *Relative time and space*

Another complication emerges when we recognise that speed is *relative*. If my walking speed is three miles per hour and I am at the airport, walking along a travelator that is moving also at 3 mph, then my speed relative to the airport concourse is 6 mph. In the same way, if I am on a train and turn on a torch, the light beam moves away from me at the speed of light. So to a lineside observer, the light beam should move at the speed of light *plus* the speed of the train. However, that total speed is obviously greater than the speed of light, which, as just discussed, is a big no-no under Relativity – we now know that the torch beam travels away from the lineside observer *also* at the speed of light. How can it be possible for both observers to see light travelling at the same speed, when they are moving with respect to each other? Speed is expressed as the amount of distance covered in a certain period of time (e.g. miles per hour) so if the speed is the same when we expect it to be different, then there must be something funny going on with distance and/or time. And indeed these are some of the consequences of Special Relativity.

Special Relativity is a perplexing place to those brought up on tidy, Newtonian physics. We find that moving clocks run slow – if someone is moving, less time passes for them than for you, standing still watching them. This is known as Time Dilation. A second consequence of Special Relativity is that moving objects are shorter; this is known as Length (or Lorentz) Contraction. These are not just theoretical claims; they have been observed in laboratory experiments many times. But it is completely contrary to the common-sense picture. Firstly, like mass, we would normally expect the length of an object to be an intrinsic property of the object itself, one of John Locke's primary qualities, and not dependent on how fast it is going. And perhaps more bizarre is the idea that different amounts of time can pass for different observers, depending on how fast they are going. Under the common-sense picture, we tend to think we can synchronise watches and then the same amount of time passes for all of us, based on some big cosmological clock in the background. It turns out that this is not so.

3. *Curved space and the Big Bang*

Following the development of more powerful telescopes in the early 20th Century, it became apparent that all the other galaxies in the universe are receding away from us, with the most distant galaxies moving away from us the fastest. This lead to the theory that the universe started c. 13.8 billion years ago with the Big Bang. This hypothesis gained mainstream acceptance in 1964, following the discovery of the Cosmic Microwave Background, the radiation that permeates the universe and can be thought of as the 'echo' of the Big Bang.

The popular picture of this idea is that instead of space being filled with all the stars and galaxies as it is today, these stars and galaxies were all squashed together in a tiny ball, which exploded into space. However, as touched on earlier, this picture isn't quite right. Rather than an amount of matter expanding into space, it turns out that it is space itself, along with the matter in it, that is expanding. A common analogy used to explain this is to think of a balloon being blown up[6]. The surface of the balloon represents space and you could draw dots on the balloon to represent galaxies. As the balloon is blown up, the galaxies move further apart because it is space itself (the surface of the balloon) that is expanding. Now that's all very well, but it immediately raises some objections. Actually, when I was doing A level physics I remember asking my teacher, 'If, in the beginning, the universe (including space itself) was only *this* big',

---

[6] The balloon analogy is helpful if the universe is finite in size, but as of the year 2023, it is not clear from the observational evidence whether this is in fact the case. For an infinite universe, it might be more helpful to think of a rubber sheet extending out to infinity in all directions, which is being stretched. 'Hold on a minute', one may say. 'If the universe is infinitely large, it must have always been infinitely large, in which case, how can it have started out really small at the Big Bang? Bear in mind that even though this rubber sheet is infinite, it has been expanding ever since the time of the Big Bang. In this context, to say that the universe was really small at the start is to say that if you take any two points on the sheet, representing the distance between two galaxies today, then at the Big Bang, they were really close together. We also note that even if the universe is infinite, and so space is 'flat' *on average*, the observational evidence still supports the claim of General Relativity that space is curved at the local level by the presence of matter.

(I was holding my thumb and forefinger about a centimetre apart), 'then what was *here*?', pointing with my other hand to a spot about a foot away.

'That's an unhelpful question', was the reply I received, which, unsurprisingly, I found very frustrating. How can space itself only be a finite size? Surely it must extend to infinity in all directions? Otherwise how does it end? Is there a brick wall at the edge of space? And even if there is, what is behind the wall?

How can something be finite (does not extend to infinity in all directions), but unbounded (there is no brick wall?). Well, one example would be the surface of the Earth (or a balloon). We can travel all over the Earth's surface and never hit a wall, but it has a finite size. If we keep moving, we just end up back where we started. We can think of a finite universe as the same but in higher dimensions i.e. if we blasted off in a space rocket and kept going in the same direction, we would (in principle) eventually end up back where we started. This sounds mind-boggling, but only because, as humans, we conceive of space in three dimensions. Imagine the amazement of someone who thought the earth was flat, who keeps going around the surface and ends up back where they started!

The earth's surface is two dimensional (it has no thickness), but is curved. Analogously, the universe is described by Einstein's general theory of relativity in terms of 'curved' space, where the curvature is caused by the presence of matter. 'Curvature' here is in a higher dimension, that we, as humans, cannot perceive directly. We can only infer that space is curved in this way, from the behaviour of the objects that we can observe. Physicists observe the bending of light from distant quasars by the curvature of space resulting from the presence of intervening galaxies. This phenomenon is known as 'gravitational lensing'.

What does all this mean for the common-sense view of the universe? Under the common-sense view, 'nothing' is the absence of objects. We say 'there is nothing in the box' to mean the box is empty – it just contains empty space[7]. Space is like the stage on which the somethings, the objects, are presented. Relativity makes us look again at space as a 'something' in its own right, which has energy and can be stretched and twisted. So again, what our common sense tells us to be the case is not always true and the 'common sense' picture of objects moving around in a fixed three-dimensional space has been shown not to be true of the real universe.

4. *The unobservable universe*

How big is the universe? Vast interstellar distances are measured in light years i.e. the distance that light can travel in a year (roughly 9.5 trillion kilometres). The nearest star to the Sun is around 4 light years away, and our galaxy, the Milky Way is around 100,000 light years across. The nearest large galaxy to the Milky Way, the Andromeda galaxy is around 2.5 million light years away, and both the Milky Way and the Andromeda galaxy form part of the local group of galaxies, the Virgo Supercluster, which is around 110 million light years across. Because light takes so long to cross these vast intergalactic distances, when we look at the Andromeda galaxy, we are not seeing it as it is now, but as it was 2.5 million years ago – looking further away is equivalent to looking back in time. The limit of what we can see therefore reflects the distance light has travelled in the 13.8 billion years since the universe became transparent[8], that is shortly after the Big Bang. This light is the Cosmic Microwave Background (CMB) touched on above. Now it might be thought that the limit of the visible universe is therefore 13.8 billion light years, but remember that in this time, space itself has been expanding. Today, by combining Einstein's General Relativity with the latest observations from the European Space Agency's Planck Collaboration, astrophysicists calculate that the actual limit of the observable universe is around 46 billion light years from earth in each direction.

---

[7] glossing over the fact that it may contain air, rather than a vacuum.

[8] Following the Big Bang, it took about 380 000 years for the universe to cool down to a temperature at which atoms can form (about 3000°C). Light was then able to travel freely – the universe became transparent.

Yet what lies beyond the observable universe? When you blow up a balloon or stretch a rubber sheet, you'll notice that with each puff, two dots that are right next to each other will only move apart very slightly, whereas dots that are further away move apart a few centimetres. So it is with the universe. The further away galaxies are from us, the faster the space between us is expanding. We cannot see the matter beyond the observable universe because the space between us has grown more rapidly than light can cross it. And the latest observational data suggests that this rate of expansion is actually increasing in such a way that light from these most distant places will never reach us.

This means more than just that we will never be able to see this part of the universe – we will never be able to interact with it in any way. In order for one event to affect another, a signal needs to pass between them – for example flicking a switch turns on a light by the flow of electric current. Similarly, 20th century physics explains the effect of forces on objects in terms of particle exchange[xxii]. But remember that under relativity, no signal can travel faster than the speed of light, which means that this part of the universe cannot have any kind of causal relationship with us. It must forever remain cut off from us. We will never be able to see it and it cannot affect us in any way.

It can therefore be seen that there are limits to what we can discover about the real universe using science. We have noted previously that a lot of the way the universe is, is hidden from us. Science tries to overcome this by making hypotheses about the way the universe is and then checking that the consequences of these hypotheses are in line with what we actually see. But we cannot check the consequences of any hypotheses about the unobservable universe because it is too far away for us to interact with it. Our understanding of the way the unobservable universe is, can only be based on speculation. We assume that it contains galaxies and stars because the observable universe that we can see contains galaxies and stars and we would expect the results of the Big Bang to be broadly similar in all parts of the universe. But like a sibling thinking about a long lost brother separated at birth, we are really just speculating and can't know any of the detail. Indeed, it raises questions about how meaningful it is to even talk of the unobservable universe. After all, if it cannot affect us in any way, then it might as well not even exist. As the Twentieth century philosopher Ludwig Wittgenstein once said, 'a nothing will serve just as well as a something about which nothing could be said'.

5. *Duality*

Many of the challenges to our common sense understanding of the universe came about through the study of light, or perhaps we should use the more technical term of electromagnet radiation. We learn at school that light is an electromagnetic wave, much like a water wave. We can drop a stone into a still pond and see the water waves spread out. Well, a light wave (or radio wave), propagates in much the same way, except that instead of there being peaks and troughs in the water, the fluctuations are in the strengths of the electric and magnetic fields. For example, the different colours of light are determined by the wavelength of the light wave (the distance between adjacent wave peaks).

The wave nature of light has been well understood ever since Scottish mathematician James Clerk Maxwell published his eponymous equations in 1865. Outside the visible spectrum lie other wavelengths of radiation that are not visible to the naked eye, but can be detected by technology, such as X-rays and radio waves. We know light is a wave because it exhibits diffraction and interference patterns, just like other waves, such as water waves. We take advantage of the wave nature of light in our technologies, modulating the amplitude (strength) and frequency of radio waves to send and receive information via radio, television and mobile phone for example.

This wave model of light was first called into question by a phenomenon known as the photoelectric effect, discovered in 1887. This is the phenomenon whereby electrons are ejected from a metal plate when light falls on it. Atoms are made of a positively charged nucleus and negatively charged electrons – these opposite charges attract and keep the electrons within the metal. However if you supply enough energy to the electrons, this gives them the speed they need to overcome the forces keeping them inside the metal and so to be ejected. The light shining on the metal provides this energy.

The puzzle of the photoelectric effect lies in the circumstances under which electrons are ejected. Under the wave model of light, we would expect that the electrons would gradually gain energy until they had sufficient energy to overcome the electric forces and get ejected; much as you would gradually get hotter if you sit next to a fire. However, what was observed is that electrons are released almost immediately and that there is a threshold frequency, below which no electrons are emitted, no matter how long you wait with the light shining.

A solution to this puzzle was offered by Albert Einstein in 1905, when he showed that this phenomenon could be explained if light was viewed as a particle. Each particle of light, known as a photon, was absorbed by the electron, giving it an instant boost of energy, equal to the energy of the photon. This explained why there was no delay – the packet of energy was absorbed straight away. This boost of energy was either sufficient or insufficient for the electron to escape the forces constraining it within the metal. Einstein showed that the energy of the photon depends only on the frequency of the light, which explains why light of too low a frequency will not be able to eject any electrons. Electrons can only absorb one photon at a time. If the energy of the photon is not sufficient to eject the electron, the photon will be released and the electron will fall back to its slower state, before absorbing the next photon. It was only by considering light as discrete particles, as 'packets' of energy which the electron absorbed one at a time, that the observed phenomenon could be explained.

So where does this leave us in our quest to understand light? Think again of throwing a stone into a pond and watching the ripples spreading out. The waves are transmitted by the motion of the water and we thought light was analogous to that, with the waves transmitted by the fluctuations of the electric and magnetic fields. Only it turns out that in some circumstances, light doesn't behave like a wave, it behaves like a particle. We know what particles are – like snooker balls on a snooker table, colliding and rebounding off each other, only smaller and in three dimensions.

So we have a new mystery: how can light be a wave in some circumstances and a particle in others? This suggests that we still don't really have a clear idea of what light actually *is*. Perhaps, someone might think, one day, we will build an even more powerful microscope and be able to actually observe a photon directly. The problem with this, as we have seen, is that microscopes typically work through the interaction of light (or electrons) with the object that we are observing. The microscope provides us with an image based on the results of such interactions, rather than directly 'seeing' the object we are inspecting. We know that when two beams of light interact, they exhibit wave behaviour resulting in phenomena such as interference patterns. But this does not give us the complete picture, as when light interacts with matter it behaves as a particle. So the idea of being able to 'see' a photon doesn't really work. 'Seeing' at the sub-atomic level can only be in the form of inspecting the effects of various sub-atomic interactions. It is the fact that light seems to have different properties depending on the circumstances of its interactions which is one of the many puzzling features of the quantum world.

Further experiments have shown that it is not just light that exhibits this strange 'duality' between being a wave and a particle. Electrons, which we usually think of as particles that orbit an atom's nucleus, were shown to exhibit wavelike properties under certain circumstances. We take advantage of the shorter 'wavelength' of electrons in the use of electron microscopes, as outlined previously when we talked about looking at atoms. The point is that although our equations of quantum mechanics and relativity can describe the behaviour of light, it seems that our everyday concepts of water waves and snooker balls are inadequate as analogues of what is actually going on at the quantum level. And indeed, what gives us cause to expect that the sub-atomic world should be describable in everyday terms? After all, our language and concepts are based on what we have experienced previously. If the subatomic world is different to anything we have seen before, then it is hardly surprising that we do not have the terms and concepts available to capture it.

The fact that at the quantum level, the properties of objects are dependent on how you interact with them leads to other strange features of the quantum world, affecting causation and measurement. These are the topics of the next section.

6. *Spontaneous Events*

In the UK there is a well-known confectionary product consisting of a malted milk centre covered by chocolate. People who have eaten a lot of these sweets are no doubt aware that although the vast majority of them provide that satisfying crunch when you bite into them, from time to time, you come across one that is chewy. How can this be, when presumably each sweet is prepared in the same way, following the same process?

One explanation might be that there are some small differences in the process, which means that some sweets end up being crunchy and some chewy. Perhaps there are small temperature differences in different parts of the oven for example, which could lead to a small number of sweets being chewy. After all, every effect has its cause, right? This is part of our common-sense picture of how the world works, and has a long tradition in western thought where it has been known as the 'principle of sufficient reason'. This culminated in the work of classical physics as laid out in Newton's Laws of motion and Maxwell's electro-magnetic theory of the late 19th century. These laws are *deterministic*. The state of the universe is a consequence of its past and the cause of its future. If we know the state of the universe now, then in theory, we can predict everything that will happen in the future.

So according to common sense, it would seem reasonable to infer that the crunchy and chewy sweets must have been prepared slightly differently. They might look the same on the outside, but actually they are different and it is this difference that determines whether a given sweet will be crunchy or chewy when you bite into it. On the other hand, perhaps you would think that a large multinational company is more than capable of producing sweets that are identical in every way. In which case, perhaps we can to turn to quantum theory for an answer!

Quantum theory would say that each sweet was prepared in the oven in an identical fashion; this being a combination (or 'superposition') of both crunchy and chewy states. Each sweet has the potential to be either crunchy or chewy, and it is the *act of biting into it*, which determines whether the sweet actually turns out to be crunchy or chewy. Before you bite into it, each sweet is exactly the same and there is no way of predicting in advance whether the sweet will be crunchy or chewy. The best we can do is to work out the probability that it will be one or the other. But the actual result that obtains is random.

This is very different from our common-sense way of thinking. A natural question might be 'why was sweet A crunchy, when sweet B was chewy? We expect to be able to get an answer to this question – every event has its cause right? But in the quantum world there is no cause. It just randomly so happened that this sweet was chewy. Determinism is lost. The classical physical laws of Newton and Maxwell in which the future is completely *determined* by the present, simply do not apply – an idea that was revolutionary when it appeared in the early 20th century. Many physicists found it hard to accept, and the idea lead Einstein to remark 'God does not play dice'.

Chapter 6

6. Inside the Strange World of Quantum and Relativistic Physics

The puzzle concerning the chocolate covered sweet described in the previous chapter relates to an aspect of quantum theory known as the Measurement Problem. Recall that under the common-sense picture, objects in the world are the way they are, irrespective of how we interact with them. A human and a dog might perceive an aeroplane differently, but the aeroplane itself is the way it is, independently of who is perceiving it. It has two wings, irrespective of whether a dog or a human is observing it. Contra Bishop Berkeley, a tree is presumed to exist in a forest even if it is unperceived by any living creature. At the quantum level, however, things are different. A quantum system in general has no meaningful properties, until they are measured.

Obviously the slightly tongue in cheek chocolate covered sweet example is intended purely to provide a 'flavour' of some of the concepts that quantum mechanics deals with and there is no serious suggestion that we need to turn to quantum theory to understand the behaviour of sweets. The manufacturer of the particular sweets in question has stated that the chewy texture can be the result of a failure to coat them properly[xxiii]. However, experiments using photons have shown this randomness at play at the quantum level. This perplexing phenomenon is perhaps best explained by again considering rays of light.

As alluded to above, Maxwell showed in the late 19th century, that light (electro-magnetic radiation) can be viewed as mutually supporting electric and magnetic fields, oscillating in a wave motion. The electric and magnetic fields oscillate in a direction perpendicular (at right-angles) to the direction of travel of the light beam, in such a way that if a light beam were to come directly towards you out of the page of this book, the electric and magnetic fields would be moving in the plane of the page. Now recall that one of the features of light, is that it can be *polarised*, that is, the electric or magnetic waves can be altered to oscillate in one direction on the page only, for example the horizontal direction or the vertical direction. This is done by means of a polarising filter.

We come across this in everyday life in the form of polarised radio and TV signals. We get a much stronger signal if the TV aerial is aligned with the direction of polarisation – maximising the ability of the electric field to drive a current through the aerial. One such polariser is a calcite crystal[xxiv]. The molecules in these crystals are lined up such that light is polarised into two separate perpendicular components. It is possible to set up conditions where light enters the crystal and is polarised such that the horizontal component is refracted in one direction and the vertical component takes a different path or channel through the crystal. Calcite crystals are able to split light into two beams because calcite is anisotropic. In such crystals, the speed of light through the crystal depends on its polarization, and so differently polarized beams refract differently and take different paths through the crystal. This results in a situation where a single unpolarised beam of light enters the crystal and two separate beams emerge out the other side, one polarised in one direction and one in the other. A second calcite crystal positioned the opposite way around can then be used to re-combine the split light beam.

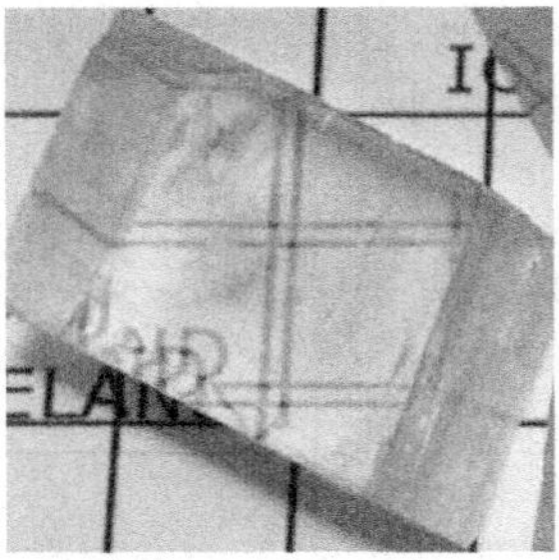

Two images produced by a calcite crystal

The interesting question is what happens in this set-up when the intensity of the light beam is so weak that only one photon passes through the crystal at a time. A photon is the smallest possible quantity of light and we know from experiments with photon counters that it is impossible to split a photon into two. We can infer in which direction the photon is polarised at the end, by recording which path it takes through a final calcite crystal which acts as a measurement device. Will it emerge from the final calcite crystal in the horizontal or vertical polarisation channel?

As with the sweets example above, it is impossible to predict this in advance. The best we can do is to work with the probability that the photon will emerge in the horizontal or vertical polarisation channel. Suppose that the probability is 50/50. With a large number of photons (i.e. a strong light beam), we would expect roughly the same number of photons to emerge from the horizontal channel as the vertical channel. i.e. the strength of the horizontally and vertically polarised beams will be the same, just as expected by classical physics. However, when we inspect the situation at the individual photon level, things get confusing. At what point does the photon's polarisation change? Presumably, it is at the point that it interacts with the calcite crystal. Experiments have been set up to test this.

Let's consider the situation above, where 45° polarised light is split into horizontal and vertical components and then recombined using a reversed calcite crystal. At the end we measure whether its polarisation is +45° or -45°. We find that for light entering the system with +45° polarisation, all the light is found to have +45° polarisation at the end. This is as we would expect in the classical case – the original +45° polarised light has been split into horizontal and vertical and then re-combined into its original form. What might we expect in the case of a single photon?

We might be tempted to reason as follows. The photon passes through the first crystal and emerges from, say, the vertical polarisation channel. When it passes through the reversed crystal, there is nothing for it to recombine with, because only one photon was released at a time. It therefore remains vertically polarised and approaches the final polariser with a 50/50 chance of being measured with either +45° or -45° polarisation. However this is not what we see. Single photons are all detected in the +45° channel of the final polariser, as if the splitting and re-combination had not occurred. To account for this, we might perhaps suggest that the reversed crystal has somehow re-instated the +45° polarisation, even though there are no other photons with which our test photon can interact. However, we find that if we block off one of the channels of the first polariser, the situation changes and the final +/-45° result is now random!

From a common-sense point of view, this makes no sense. How can blocking off the exit from one channel, through which the photon doesn't pass, affect the photon that goes through the completely separate other channel? What this experiment shows, is that for some strange reason, the calcite crystal only impacts the photon's polarisation *if it is used as a measuring device*. In the first scenario, the photon's polarisation was only measured after it had passed through the two crystals, so it was as if these two crystals weren't even there. In the second scenario however, by blocking off one of the channels, we have in effect measured the polarisation of all emerging photons – if we block the exit of the horizontal channel, we know that all emerging photons have vertical polarisation at that point. We shouldn't be surprised therefore to find that outcome of the final +/-45° measurement is random.

This is one of the key points of the standard interpretation of the results of quantum experiments – it is meaningless to ascribe properties to quantum objects until they are measured. It is important to take this literally. We are not saying merely that we can't *know* the properties of quantum objects until they are measured. We are in effect saying that these quantum objects do not have any definitive properties until these properties are measured. We are saying that it is the act of measuring that impacts the photon.

This again, is a radical departure from classical physics. A sweet cannot be classified as crunchy or chewy until we bite into it. A photon cannot be thought of as horizontally or vertically polarised until we measure it. As Alastair Rae puts it in his book *Quantum Physics: Illusion or Reality*, the only information we can have about the quantum world is obtained from these measurements, which always have an effect on the system being measured. It is therefore pointless to ascribe properties to an isolated quantum system, as we can never know what these are: real physical properties are possessed only by the combined system of the microscopic object plus measuring apparatus. According to Niels Bohr, one of the pioneers of quantum theory in the early 20th century, it is incorrect to speculate on what the photon polarisation was before the measurement, as any attempt to measure it will interfere with it.

When scientists look to measure which path the photon took through the crystal, they use a detector. They observe dots on a screen, reinforcing the view of photon as particles – little snooker balls, tracking particular paths through space. But this view of the underlying structure of the universe is not compatible with the experimental result above, where shutting off one channel affects a photon that is ostensibly in a different channel. Instead, it appears that photons are somehow able to have an influence over a wide area, yet behave like point particles when detected. Our 'common-sense' view of a series of discrete objects tracking paths through space and time, independently of any observer is seen to be inadequate to describe events at the quantum level. Or to put it more bluntly – the common-sense view is just plain wrong.

The majority of us perhaps find the experimental results and the quantum mechanical explanation of the measurement problem bewildering when we first encounter them. I remember at university, my tutor telling me that quantum physics is something that you get used to, but not really something that you ever make sense of. Quantum mechanics forces us to question the very foundations of what we believe to be true about the world around us. We traditionally think of a clear distinction between how things are, and our knowledge of how things are. Things are a certain way, independently of whether we have knowledge of this or not. Quantum mechanics blurs this distinction. It says that it is not true to think that it could be the case that things are a certain way (e.g. a photon is horizontally or vertically polarised) and we don't know what that is. Rather, it is the act of finding out how things are that determines how things are.

What does it mean to say that quantum objects only have real properties once they are measured? Measuring requires an observer to do the measuring, otherwise the measuring equipment is just part of the quantum system. If we think back to John Locke's distinction between Primary and Secondary qualities, this might suggest that *all* the qualities of a quantum object are secondary. A quantum object has no qualities that are an inherent part of the object itself – it only has the potential to have certain qualities. The qualities only become real features when measured by an observer. We might also be reminded of Bishop Berkeley's claim that 'To be is to be perceived'. Before an object is perceived (measured) it just exists in a quantum superposition of potential states, but has no real features. And does this idea just apply to quantum objects or to all objects? If I measure my brother to be six feet (182 cm) tall, then surely he was also six feet tall in the moment before I measured him? Yet, if this theory only applies to quantum objects, then where is the line between a quantum object and other objects? It is the seemingly absurd results of trying to apply these quantum ideas to the everyday world that are illustrated by the famous thought experiment of Schrödinger's Cat.

Schrödinger's cat sits in a sealed box together with a photon and a polariser. If the photon emerges in the horizontal channel, it triggers a gun which kills the cat. Schrödinger is upset, but fortunately this is only a thought experiment. If the photon emerges in the vertical channel, the cat survives. Now according to the standard interpretation of quantum mechanics, and in line with what we have been discussing above, the path the photon has taken through the polariser cannot be said to have any meaningful reality until it is measured. And consequently, whether the gun has been fired or not cannot be said to have any meaningful reality until it also is measured. This won't be until we open the box. So it seems that until we open the box and observe which path the photon has taken, the cat is neither alive nor dead, but in a kind of suspended animation. At least from our point of view. From the cat's point of view, it knows perfectly well whether or not it is alive or dead – or so we might think. The crucial point here is that it is not merely the case that we don't *know* whether the cat is alive or dead. It's that according to quantum physics, the cat really is neither alive nor dead until we open the box. Yet such a conclusion, and this was Schrödinger's point, seems ridiculous.

Now quantum mechanics is a very successful scientific theory, when judged in terms of accurately predicting the outcomes of experiments, and much of modern technology, for example the microchip, relies on quantum results. However it is thought experiments like Schrödinger's Cat that lead many to think that it must be fundamentally flawed as a description of how the world actually *is*. We should not be afraid to doubt. Newtonian Mechanics was a successful model for hundreds of years, before it was ultimately shown not to be correct. Perhaps in the quantum world too, there is another 'deeper' theory to be discovered that describes what the world is really like.

Space and Time

It isn't just the nature of causation and the impact of measurement, that were called into question by the advent of 20th Century physics. The second result of the new physics that we will look at in more detail concerns the nature of space and time. The common-sense picture of the physical universe starts with space. This space contains objects. Someone then presses 'play' and time starts and these objects all move about in space as time passes. However, it was recognised as early as 1883 by the German physicist Ernst Mach, that this view was not wholly scientific. It was an assumption about the way the universe was, rather than one implied by the empirical evidence. In fact, 20th Century Relativity tells us that space and time are relative to the observer; that is to say time and space may behave differently for you than they do for me. One of the first major challenges to this 'common sense' view of the universe came about with the Michelson and Morley experiments of 1881 and 1887, designed to investigate the effect of the earth's motion on the speed of light.

As mentioned already, the wave nature of light had been well established by the late 1800's, through various experiments and underpinned by Maxwell's theory of electro-magnetism. But there was continuing debate around the medium that supports light waves. Water waves travel by the up and down motion of the water. Sound waves travel through the vibrations of molecules in the air. But what is it that allows light waves to travel through empty space? The answer was a hypothetical substance called the 'aether' and the Michelson-Morley experiments were designed to measure the effect of the Earth's passage through it on the measured speed of light.

What was the idea behind the experiment? Imagine you are at sea in a strong wind. If you are on a boat heading into the wind, you will feel the force of these waves crashing into you at a much greater relative speed than if the wind is behind you. The Michelson-Morley experiments used this principal, with a beam of light in place of the water waves and the earth in place of the boat. The experiment investigated how the measured speed of light differed when the beam of light was in line with the path of the Earth as it travelled around the sun, versus when then beam of light was perpendicular to the path of the Earth. The earth is around eight light minutes from the sun, and takes a year to complete one orbit. This means that it is hurtling around the sun at around one hundred thousand kilometres per hour. But this is still only a tiny fraction of the speed of light, which travels at around one billion kilometres per hour. Technology at the time was not sophisticated enough to distinguish between the expected speeds of the two different light beams, but by cleverly allowing the parallel beam to intersect the perpendicular beam, it was possible to detect differences in speed by inspecting the interference pattern.

However, disappointingly for all concerned at the time, no difference in speed was detected, and this left a great puzzle. It was as if the waves hit you at the same speed, irrespective of whether you are travelling upwind or downwind. How could that be?

The puzzle was solved by Albert Einstein and formalised in his theory of Special Relativity, published in 1905. Einstein's genius was to avoid looking for complex explanations as to why the results of the experiment were different to what was expected, but to take the results at face value and use that to challenge our preconceived notions about how the universe works.

Einstein said that if the experiment showed that the speed of light was the same for all observers, then this was because it was indeed the case. It doesn't matter what speed you are travelling. It doesn't matter whether the light is emitted by a laser in a laboratory here on earth or by a star travelling at millions of miles per hour in a different direction – the speed of light as detected by any observer[9] will always be the same. This is the first postulate of Einstein's theory of Special Relativity.

If this is the case, then the implications are startling. As we know from school, speed is just a measure of the amount of distance covered in a certain amount of time, e.g. the number of kilometres per hour. If the speed of light is always the same, irrespective of the speed of the observer, what does this imply for the distance travelled or the time taken?

Let's first imagine someone with a lamp standing in the middle of a freight container. This person removes a covering from the lamp and beams of light head off in all directions. In particular, one beam of light heads towards the front wall and one to the rear wall. Because this person is standing in the middle of the container, the distance travelled by the light from the source to the container walls is the same. The speed of the light

---

[9] In a vacuum. We learn at school that the passage of light is slowed by different media - for example rainbows are the result of different frequencies (colours) of light being slowed by different amounts as light passes through the thicker water droplets.

is the same and so the light beams strike the front and rear walls at the same time.

Now let's imagine what happens if the container is being pulled along at a constant speed in a freight train. Scientists have long recognised that without being able to see the outside world passing by, there is no way of telling whether you are moving at a constant speed or whether you are at rest. For example, if you imagine being in a lift, you cannot tell if you are moving until you feel the force of the lift slowing down as it arrives at the destination floor. The second postulate of Special Relativity formalises this. For all inertial frames of reference (i.e. for all environments travelling at a constant speed), the laws of physics are the same (i.e. you cannot tell any difference between these environments).

So for this person in the container, whether or not it is being pulled along in a train makes no difference. They can't know whether the container is moving or not, the ride is so smooth! And the light strikes both walls at the same time, either way. But what is the situation for an observer standing in a Position of Safety on the lineside? When the cover is removed and the light is released, the container walls are moving. The rear wall is moving forward, so the light that strikes this wall will have travelled a shorter distance than the light that has to catch up with the front wall that is moving away from the point where the light was emitted.

Now, pre-Einstein, this additional bit of complexity makes no difference to the end result. From the perspective of our lineside observer, we would expect the light to be travelling at the speed of light *plus* the speed of the train. So although the light heading towards the front of the container has to travel further, it is travelling faster. And therefore we would still expect the light to strike the front and rear walls of the container at the same time[10]. The conclusion is different however, when we recognise that the

[10] This can be demonstrated more precisely by considering the situation where instead of shining a light, the person in the container rolls a ball. They roll two balls, one towards the front of the container and one towards the back, releasing them both just as they, stationed in the middle of the container, pass the lineside observer. They release the balls at the same speed – the speed that the train is moving. The actual speed of the balls, relative to the observer, is the speed at which they were released plus the speed of the container. The ball rolled towards the back of the container is therefore actually not moving at all relative to our lineside

speed of light is the same for all observers. For our lineside observer, the two beams of light are travelling at the same speed c, but the beam heading towards the back of the container has a shorter distance to travel. This means for our lineside observer, the back of the container is struck *before* the front of the container, whereas for our man in the container, both walls are struck at the same time! *Events that are simultaneous in one frame of reference are not simultaneous in another!*

And it doesn't end with beams of light. We have seen that speed is intimately linked with distance and time, and so the only way two observers can experience the same speed of light, even though they are moving relative to each other, is if distance and time are also affected. This can be seen as follows. Let's say one of the light beams hits the rear of the container, just as the rear of the container is passing a tree on the lineside. And let's say the other beam of light hits the front of the container just as the front of the container is entering a tunnel. From the point of view of our man on the train, these two events happen at the same time. The front of the train enters the tunnel just as the rear of the train passes the tree. The distance between the tree and the tunnel entrance is, say 21 feet, so we know the container is 21 feet long.

However, our lineside observer sees the light strike the rear of the container before the other beam strikes the front of the container. So the rear of the container passes the tree *before* the front of the container enters the tunnel! This is pretty earth-shattering stuff, because it has implications for our notions of a single absolute truth. According to Special Relativity, person A could tell the court that the two events happened at the same time, and person B could swear that they did not, and they could *both be right*. But even stranger than that, the only way

---

observer, whereas the ball rolling towards the front of the container is travelling at twice the speed of the train, relative to the lineside observer. As the ball rolled backwards is not moving relative to the lineside observer, the time taken will be the time it takes for the back end of the container of length l, travelling at speed v, to reach the observer: 0.5 l /v (as time = distance / speed, and the distance is half a container length). The ball rolled forward is travelling at twice the speed of the train (2v), relative to the lineside observer and will strike the front of the container at time t, position r. r can be determined by considering the position of the ball when it strikes the front of the container at time t: r = speed x time = 2vt. r can also be determined by considering the position of the front of the container when it is struck by the ball at time t: r = 0.5l+vt (The front of the container is half a length (0.5l) in front of the ball when the ball is released and travels a further distance vt before being struck by the ball). Combining these, we get 2vt = 0.5l+vt or t = 0.5l/v, which is the same time that the other ball hits the back of the container.

that the rear of the train can pass the tree before the front of the container enters the tunnel is if the container is *shorter* than the distance between the tree and the tunnel entrance! This phenomenon is known as 'length contraction' or 'Lorentz contraction' – objects are shorter when moving!

We are again reminded of John Locke's distinction between primary and secondary qualities. It turns out that an object's size, something that we thought should be an intrinsic property of the object itself, is actually subjective and will be different for different observers.

The second significant consequence of the postulates of special relativity is known as Time Dilation – moving clocks run more slowly. What does it mean to say that moving clocks run slowly? Do they measure 10 seconds, when actually 20 seconds have gone by? Or is it like with a terrible accident when things happen in slow motion? Each second takes longer to go by? But isn't that more about our perception of time, rather than time itself?

Our perception of the passage of time, or how long it takes a second to pass, may be different in different circumstances or for different people and we explore this further later. However, in physics, in order to be able to agree a standard for how much time is passing, a unit of time, e.g. the 'second', is defined in terms of regular occurrences in the physical world. It used to be defined as the length of time it takes the earth to rotate (1 day) divided by 24 hours, divided by 60 minutes, divided by 60 seconds. However, since 1967, it has been defined with reference to the frequency of light emitted by a transition between two particular energy levels of a cesium-133 atom, as this is more regular. Therefore a clock is anything that produces regular repetitive motion. Modern watches measure time by the vibration of a quartz crystal. To measure time, we count the repetitions. For example, we could consider the earth to be a clock. Count the number of revolutions in order to measure the number of days.

Now we can understand Time Dilation by imagining a clock in a container. This clock works by bouncing a beam of light between the side walls of the container, which are, say, 3 metres apart. Let's *define* each repetition, the time it takes for the light beam to travel from one wall to the other, to be ten nanoseconds. Our man in the container doesn't know if he is at rest or moving on a train – it is all the same to him. Let's say his container is on a moving train. We also have stationary container clocks at each station. A horn sounds when the train leaves the station and we start counting repetitions. When the train gets to its destination station, another horn sounds and let's say the station clocks have performed 100 billion repetitions. How many repetitions will the clock on the train have performed? From the point of view of our lineside observer, the beam of light has to move diagonally, in order to stay with the train, as well as crossing to the other side of the container, and so it travels further per repetition than for the clock at rest in the station. As it has to travel further per repetition, each repetition will take longer and it will perform fewer repetitions between the two horn sounds, than the station clocks. As time is measured by repetitions, this means that fewer seconds – less time – has passed for our man on the train, or to put it another way *moving clocks run slow!*

If this feels like a trick, it is probably because we are used to thinking in pre-Einstein terms. Our man on the train can't tell if he is moving or at rest, so from his perspective, the light beam is only travelling the short 3 metres per repetition. Pre-Einstein, we might say that although it is true that he is only *seeing* it travel the short distance, the light beam is *actually* travelling a greater distance each time. It therefore takes longer to cross the container, and so will appear to be travelling more slowly. So although it is true to say each repetition takes longer, this doesn't mean that less time has passed. But we now know that this reasoning is flawed! The key point is that the speed of light is the *same* in the moving container as it is outside – three hundred million metres per second. For both our man in the container and our man at the station, when they look at their respective clocks, the time for a repetition is the time it takes light travelling at 300 million metres per second to cross 3 metres – 10 nanoseconds. Yet from the point of view of the man on the lineside, fewer repetitions – fewer nanoseconds – will have been experienced between stations by the train clock than by the lineside clock. Less time has passed for the moving clock on the train.

This is astounding! The common-sense idea of a single time, the same for everyone, flowing onwards, independently of the objects in the universe was always just speculation, and, as we have seen, wrong. I mentioned briefly earlier that if a different amount of time passes for me than does for you, or if events that are simultaneous for me are not simultaneous for you, then this has implications for our notions of a single absolute truth. Now you might argue that it is over-egging the pudding and point out instead that there is a single absolute truth, namely the truth described by Special Relativity that lengths and periods of time can be quantified and are dependent on the observers. However, what we can and should draw from this debate is that our language and our thinking about the universe often pre-supposes fundamental concepts that are unthinkingly assumed to apply. We need to be mindful that the way we conceptualise the universe may not be right and similarly, our understanding of what is universally true and what is not is open to future challenge.

20th century physics made great strides in overcoming our naïve common-sense notions regarding the world around us, but how confident can we be that the ideas of relativity and quantum physics are themselves not fundamentally flawed? Ideally, we would have a description of the physical universe that combines all these ideas into a single coherent framework. In the next chapter I'll take a look at how close we are to such a theory and whether this would be the panacea that might be hoped for.

Chapter 7

7. The True Laws of Reality

The development of General Relativity and Quantum Mechanics in the early 20th century has proven to be a great step forward in the furthering of our understanding of the world around us, with both theories standing the test of time. To date, all the experimental and observational evidence has been in line with their predictions, despite numerous attempts to show their predictions to be false. And yet while our understanding can be said to be further forward in terms of the universe's *behaviour,* our confidence in understanding the actual structure of the universe and the nature of the objects in it has been thoroughly shaken.

By the latter half of the 19th century, Newton's laws of motion and the theories of gravitation and electromagnetism appeared to give a complete description of the behaviour of natural phenomena. While there were details and implications to be worked through, most people believed that at a fundamental level, the nature of the universe was understood. However, as we have seen in chapters 5 and 6, this commonsense picture that stood at the time has since been thoroughly undermined. Today, space, the stage on which our Newtonian objects perform, is now seen to be a thing in its own right, with energy that can be stretched and twisted. Rather than existing in the three dimensions we are familiar with, we now say that it has at least four dimensions and indeed, maybe many more, if some of the more modern string theories are to be believed. Time, bizarrely, can be different for different people.

Likewise, objects that inhabit this space and time are also a lot more difficult to get to grips with than we previously thought. Starting with the universe itself which, although usually presented as vanishingly small at the time of the Big Bang, may also have been infinitely large! The objects in it might be waves but also might be particles depending on their circumstances. Or perhaps it is the case that they aren't actually anything at all until we measure (interact) with them. When they do interact with each other, usual notions of causation need not apply! Spontaneous, uncaused events are to be expected.

If this is all too much to cope with, you might wonder, well why don't we go back to our common-sense picture? This works well enough every day, so why tie ourselves in knots with all this relativistic quantum strangeness? After all, our brains evolved to see the world using the common-sense picture of discrete material objects in three dimensional space, persisting through time and causally interacting with each other. And this is fine, but it pays to bear in mind that the common-sense picture is just that – a picture. A bit like telling small children that babies are delivered by storks, it is a way of looking at the universe which makes it easy to make sense of; easy to navigate, but this isn't actually the way things are.

A trickier question that we might ask though, is that even given that Quantum Mechanics and General Relativity provide a better description of how the universe behaves than the classical theories of Newton and Maxwell, can we be sure that they give a true description of the way the universe is? Could it be that these theories are also wrong and that in some important way, the common-sense picture is right, albeit needing to be re-expressed in terms of a different theory that more accurately reflects the observational and experimental evidence? Partially, at least, the answer to this question is 'No'. The fact that space and time are different for different observers has been experimentally verified many times. Furthermore, in 2022, the Nobel Prize for physics was awarded to John

Clauser, Alain Aspect and Anton Zeilinger for showing that even if Quantum Mechanics is wrong, any replacement theory must go against the common-sense picture, in that the results of an experiment in one location can instantly determine the result of an observation in another location, even though there is no interaction between them (in the same way, as discussed earlier, that shutting off one channel in our calcite crystal affected the polarisation of the photon despite the fact that it didn't pass through that channel)[xxv].

So, in order to answer the question of whether our modern theories of physics give a true description of the way the universe is, we can start by asking if there are any observable phenomena that cannot be explained by our existing theories – anomalies like the photoelectric effect (discussed in chapter 5) which couldn't be explained by the wave model of light. Perhaps the most high profile mysteries of the universe still to be explained are 'dark matter' and 'dark energy'.

Dark Matter[xxvi]

The concept of 'Dark matter' was proposed by Fritz Zwicky in the 1930s when it was noted that a cluster of galaxies known as the Coma cluster were orbiting at a speed which meant that each galaxy should have flown off into space – much like if you have a ball on the end of a rope whirling around in a circle and then let go. It is the tension in the rope that pulls the ball in towards the centre and keeps it from flying off. In the same way, gravity keeps our planets in orbit around the sun and the galaxies in question orbiting around the cluster. We know from both Newton and Einstein's laws of gravitation, that the more massive two bodies are, the stronger the force of gravitational attraction between them. Based on the speed at which the galaxies are rotating, the gravitational force needed to keep them in orbit in the cluster is much more than that expected to be present, given their masses.

How can this be explained? Well the concept of 'dark matter' results from the idea that scientists have not correctly accounted for all the mass that is present. After all, not all matter is visible. We can detect the stars because they emit radiation – they shine. Could the additional matter be items such as planets or interstellar dust? Yet, investigations into what happened around the time of the Big Bang have revealed that this could not be the answer, based on the following reasoning. We know that the universe started with the Big Bang and has been expanding ever since. Around three minutes after the Big Bang, the temperature of the universe had cooled to a mere 1 billion Kelvin[11]. At this time, protons and neutrons were present and were colliding together to form light elements in a process called nucleosynthesis. For example, a helium nucleus is formed when two protons and two neutrons fuse together. Exactly which elements could be formed depended on the density of matter at this time – the more protons and neutrons there were, the more collisions there could have been, which would impact the relative amounts of each of these elements. Physicists can analyse the relative amounts of these light elements present in the universe today[12] and therefore infer the density of baryonic matter (broadly, protons and neutrons) at the time of this nucleosynthesis. This enables them to tell how much matter should be present in the universe today. This analysis indicates that there is about twice as much baryonic matter than we would expect, based purely on what we can see. However, the motions of the galaxies in the universe suggests that there should be around ten times more matter than we can see!

How can this discrepancy be resolved? Either our theories of gravitation are wrong, or our common conception of matter consisting mainly of protons and neutrons[13], is not the full story. Unwilling to abandon gravitational theories that have proven so successful in other respects, physicists take the idea of this additional matter seriously and call it 'dark matter'. Because we cannot 'see' dark matter, it is believed not to interact at all using the electromagnetic force, and so large projects are underway to try to detect it by other means. Since the 1930s, the concept of dark

---

[11] Which is also roughly a billion degrees Centigrade

[12] Physicists look at the composition of gas clouds between galaxies so that the data is not distorted by the actions of stars which convert hydrogen into helium through nuclear fusion and generate heavier elements when exploding in a supernova. A key element in this work is deuterium – a form of hydrogen with a nucleus consisting of one proton and one neutron. This element is destroyed inside stars but is present in interstellar clouds.

[13] Note that electrons are around 2,000 times lighter than protons and neutrons

matter has been used to explain other anomalies and dark matter is currently thought to make up about 27% of the universe, with only around 5% of the universe being normal matter (all the stuff we actually know about). The other 68% of the universe is so called 'dark energy'.

Dark Energy

Like dark matter, dark energy fills a gap between theory and observation. We noted above that the universe started with the Big Bang and has been expanding ever since. Since all the matter in the universe (stars, galaxies, planets, dust etc) attract each other through gravity, it was expected that the rate of the universe's expansion gradually slows over time; the gravitational attraction between the stars acting as a brake on the hurtling motion caused by the initial explosion. However, when the rate of expansion was first measured in 1998, it was found that it was actually speeding up! This implies that there is something stronger than gravity, acting against it to push the universe apart. This energy is different from anything that had been considered before. It is not the energy of radiation or the energy inherent in matter. It has been characterised as the energy inherent in empty space, and is also known as 'dark energy'. Now this can be allowed for in Einstein's General theory of Relativity by adjusting a parameter known as the Cosmological Constant. Yet the problem is that the value of this constant predicted by Quantum Field Theory is nowhere near the value implied by observational measurements.

Work to solve the mysteries of dark matter and dark energy is ongoing, but what is clear is that the theories we have currently do not give us a complete picture of the workings of the universe. Although the holy grail of physics, to come up with a 'Theory of Everything', providing a full description of how the universe is configured behind the scenes, remains elusive, progress has been made in recent decades.

A Theory of Everything

As the 20th century progressed, physicists continued to develop quantum mechanics and this led to a culmination in the 1970s with the development of the Standard Model of particle physics. The Standard Model describes the interactions and behaviours related to three of the four fundamental forces of nature – electromagnetism and the strong and weak nuclear forces. Of course, a scientific theory is just a theory until its predictions are confirmed by experiment. One key element of the Standard Model is the Higgs Field, which permeates space and gives subatomic particles their mass. The carrier particle for the Higgs Field is the Higgs boson, so finding traces of this postulated entity in high energy particle collision experiments was considered a key test for the Standard Model. In 2013, it was announced that the particle had been found using the Large Hadron Collider at CERN in Switzerland, and Peter Higgs and François Englert, who had proposed the Higgs mechanism received Nobel prizes[xxvii].

Following on from the arrival of the Standard Model, the challenge was on to expand it further to incorporate gravity – the fourth fundamental force of nature. As discussed above, our best theory of gravity currently, is Einstein's General Relativity, but this does not describe gravity in quantum terms. Now at this stage, one might ask, do we really need a unifying theory? Could we not just say that the Standard Model and General Relativity together is a complete description of the universe? The problem is that the Standard Model and General Relativity are not consistent; that is, they don't characterise the universe in the same way. And if they characterise the universe in different ways, they can't both be a true description of the way the universe actually *is*.

For practical purposes, inconsistencies in the two great theories of physics are not normally a problem, as they are used in different situations. Gravity, for example, affects bodies with mass, but gravity is also the weakest of the four forces and therefore is typically only needed for massive objects like stars and galaxies, where the gravitational force is dominant. Conversely, for practical purposes, at the subatomic quantum level, the other forces dominate, and gravity can be ignored. However, there *are* situations where the scale is small, but gravitational forces dominate – situations where a huge amount of matter is packed into a tiny space. Examples are black holes and the situation at the dawn of the universe i.e. conditions at the time of the Big Bang. In order to understand these properly, we need a quantum theory of gravity, ideally as part of a theory that unifies all four of the fundamental forces of nature – something that begins to approach being a Theory of Everything.

Following the development of the Standard Model of particle physics, physicists have been working on a unifying theory and perhaps the most well-known of these is 'String Theory'[xxviii]. So is String Theory the ultimate answer to life, the universe and everything? There are a whole family of String theories, which all purport to provide a theoretical framework to subsume both the Standard Model and General Relativity, but how do we know which one, if any, are right?

I noted earlier that an atom was one ten thousandth of a micron or 10^{-10} m across. The size of the nucleus of an atom is around 5 orders of magnitude below that – 10^{-15} m. The strings postulated by string theory lie behind particles such as electrons and photons and we traditionally see these particles as being so small that they can be treated as a point with no size[14]. These strings are of the order of the Planck length – 10^{-34} m. To get a sense how small that is, if an atom were the size of the solar system, a string would be the size of an atom![15]. This implies we have no hope of ever being able to see these strings directly. So as we noted with the Standard Model and Higgs Boson, in order to corroborate a Theory of Everything, we need a prediction which can be subjected to experimental test. Unfortunately, so far it has proven extremely difficult to come up with an experiment that can produce definitive results. Simple string theory models disagree with experiment and the class of those that one is forced to examine to avoid this, is too large to be predictive.

---

[14] When they are not being treated as waves – see Section 5

[15] $10^{-10} / 10^{-34} = 10^{24}$. Diameter of the solar system is 10^{14} m.

This is a shame, as it would be handy to have a robust Theory of Everything as a starting point in investigating whether God exists. After all, if God exists, then God is part of everything and so a theory of everything should, in principle, be able to predict the existence of God. Now some may argue that when we say 'everything' in this context, we mean everything in the universe. Whereas God, surely, is outside the universe. God *must* be outside the universe because he created it and he couldn't have created himself. So it would seem that God exists separately from his creation. In which case, might one argue that a Theory of Everything could quite reasonably describe the behaviour of everything in the universe, without having anything to say about whether or not God exists?

However, arguing that our theory of how the universe works does not apply to God, raises the question of how then God interacts with his creation. If everything in the universe can be explained in naturalistic terms, without any outside influence, then we are left with the 'thin' God of the Epicureans, mentioned in Chapter 3. This is God as 'divine watchmaker'. He created the world and then stepped back, admiring his handywork, with no further involvement. This obviously means prayers have no effect, which is not the God most of us are thinking of when asking the question of whether God exists. It also raises questions about Heaven and Hell. Should a Theory of Everything predict the existence of Heaven and Hell (perhaps as parallel universes?) or is it limited to a description of 'our' universe? It may reasonably be pointed out that it is not really a theory of Everything if there are some things (God) that lie outside its domain. Perhaps a true theory of everything would cover both God (if God exists) and his creation, thereby providing a mechanism by which prayers are granted and the soul ascends to Heaven / is cast into the fiery pits of Hell.

Now some theists have looked to get around the difficulty of explaining how God interacts with his creation by suggesting that he primarily acts through people. God acts in the world by providing guidance to people in the choices that they make. This wheeze exploits the fact that although we can predict a lot about the universe using our understanding of the laws of nature, as touched on earlier, the question of Free Will remains unresolved. If the laws of nature only describe the material world, then perhaps, like God, our souls are also outside the domain of these laws and our choices are genuinely free. Debate continues over whether there is a soul, sitting in the brain, existing independently of the body, which may continue to exist after the body dies.

The view that soul and body are separate is known as 'dualism'. The approach appears in Plato's writings over 2000 years ago and retains tremendous influence in popular culture to this day. However dualism is not popular among academics, who ask difficult questions like 'how does the soul interact with the body?' This is perhaps analogous to the question of how God acts in the universe. Theists may therefore not need to restrict God's actions in the world to influencing people's choices. It could be argued that while it is not clear how we, as conscious subjects, control our bodies – how does my desire to lift my arm result in my arm actually moving? – it is nonetheless clear that the mind does control the body. And so, while we struggle to find a mechanism for how God acts in the world, that does not mean to say that he cannot act in it.

Researchers have also pointed to the fact that changes in our bodies affect our mind and our personalities. For example, if we are in an accident and suffer brain damage, this not only impacts our body, but also changes our personality and the way we see the world. If our soul is separate from our body, this raises questions about how our soul can change over time – is it affected by changes in our body? If not, if our soul is unchanging, then our soul is something different from our personality and mental states, so what actually is it? The picture of the soul in popular culture of a ghost, retaining the personality of the individual at the point of death is problematic if a body is necessary for a personality.

An increasingly popular conception of consciousness is the idea that it is purely a manifestation of systems that surpass a certain level of complexity. Some consequences of this view are that there is no life after death and that robots could theoretically be self-conscious, if complex enough. Some revisionist views of Christianity see God in a similar way[xxix].

In the same way that the soul is not separate from the body, God is not separate from the world, but rather a different way of looking at it. Perhaps a future robust Theory of Everything would help. Does it contain 'soul' particles, or at least allow for some kind of ghost-like entity that can ride the brain and interact with it, while at the same time having an independent existence of their own? In the same way, perhaps if we understood the true nature of reality, through a theory of everything, it would provide a mechanism for how prayer works and perhaps even open doors to understanding how a soul can transition to Heaven.

Deductive and Inductive Reasoning

There are perhaps some who may find the above considerations uncomfortable. As noted earlier, asking for firm evidence for the existence of God removes the requirement for belief. Is it not the case that the benefits of piousness are a reward for faith? Might it be said that those who are late to the party and only join once doubt about God's existence is removed, haven't really earned the right to be there? Following this line of thinking, rejecting the findings of science where they conflict with religious beliefs can be seen as a test of faith, and rejecting science as a badge of honour. We noted examples such as Creationism earlier, of people saying 'Science doesn't know everything'. In such circles, Science is viewed as a misguided endeavour that is not to be trusted. In response, we might suggest that actually science is nothing more than our everyday efforts to find out about the world, carried out in line with some guiding principles to try to minimise the likelihood of going astray. It is nothing mysterious – it is just what we would call normal rational behaviour in the 21st century in understanding the world around us.

Consider, for example, what you would do if sitting at home and the lights suddenly went out. Perhaps you might first check if other lights in the house are working. If they are not, you might check the circuit breakers on the fuse board. If they have not tripped, you might look out the window to see if the neighbour's lights are on or phone a friend to see if they have power. And if they are off too, you may conclude that there has been a power cut. You might look to corroborate this by using your phone to check for news from the electricity supplier. Here, the scientific method has been applied – a phenomenon has been observed that is in need of an explanation (the lights have gone out). A hypothesis has been proposed to explain it (the circuit breaker has cut the power to the lights). An experiment was devised to test this (the circuit breaker was observed not to have tripped). An alternative hypothesis was proposed (there has been a power cut).

Having said that, can we be sure that science is the true or only path to knowledge? I said earlier that we use the techniques of science to discover how the world is, beyond what we can immediately perceive, but is that really what we achieve through scientific endeavour? Perhaps it is time to consider the actual techniques of science in a bit more detail. Science makes use of two forms of reasoning in order to make progress – inductive and deductive reasoning.

Deductive Reasoning

Let's take deductive reasoning first. This kind of reasoning allows us to combine various facts and rules about a system in order to establish other facts. Let's look at a simple system below, which shows a battery powered lamp, triggered by a switch.

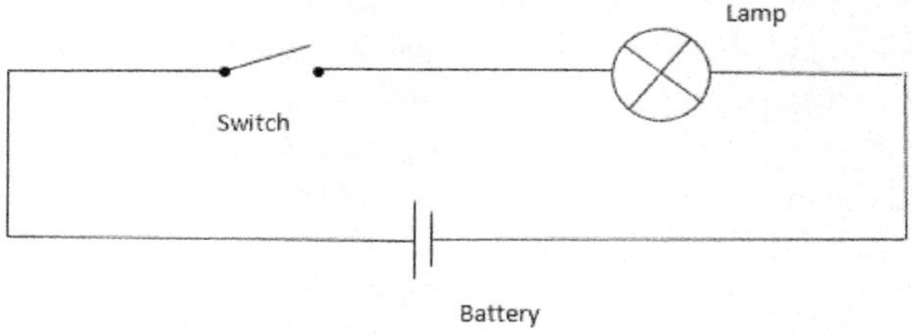

We have the following premises:-
A: If the switch is closed, then the lamp will be lit
B: The switch is closed

From premises A and B, I can *deduce* that C: the lamp will be lit. This form of deduction is known as *modus ponens*. Alternatively, I could reason as follows:-

A: If the switch is closed, then the lamp will be lit
B: The lamp is not lit

Therefore
C: The switch is not closed.

This form of deduction is known as *modus tollens*. Note straightaway here that the truth of the conclusion depends on the truth of the premise. If the lamp is not lit, does this have to mean that the switch is not closed? Could there by other explanations? What about if the battery has failed? If the battery is flat, this calls into question premise A, that if I close the switch, the lamp will light. I may decide that I need a more rigorous premise A. How about
A: If the switch is closed *and* the battery is charged, *then* the lamp will be lit.

Again, can we be sure this premise is true? What about if the connections are loose? So although deductive reason gives us a guaranteed path from premise to conclusion, the truth or otherwise of the premises needs careful consideration.

Inductive Reasoning

The alternative kind of reasoning works in the opposite direction – starting with individual facts and building up to form general rules about a system. We might take as an example a series of dominos, all stood on end – a domino rally. We notice that the first domino falls over, and as it does, it comes into contact with the second domino. This domino then falls over, and as it does, it comes into contact with the third domino. The third domino then falls over, as it does, coming into contact with the fourth domino and so on. We observe that whenever a falling domino comes into contact with a standing domino, the standing domino falls and this happens without fail until the end of the series.

We infer from this that the falling domino *causes* the standing domino to fall. This is a conceptual jump. We have only observed a finite number of cases, but we are claiming that this will be true in all such cases. We have observed a correlation – a preceding domino falling is correlated with the subsequent domino falling – and assumed a causal connection. But, as Hume pointed out, we cannot be sure that this causal connection exists. For all we know, the next time we knock a domino over, it might fall right through the subsequent domino, leaving it standing in place!

This process of generalising from observations of particular cases to speculation regarding general rules which apply in all cases is known as *inductive* reasoning. In contrast to deductive reasoning, it does not have that certainty in moving from the start to the end position. This is often famously illustrated by the example of the inductivist turkey.

The turkey found that, on his first day at the turkey farm, he was fed. Being a good inductivist turkey he did not jump to conclusions. He waited until he collected a large number of observations, and made these observations under a wide range of circumstances, on weekdays and at the weekend, on warm days and cold days. Each day he added another observation to his list. Finally he was satisfied that he had collected a sufficient number of observations to inductively infer that "I am fed every day". However one morning, rather than being fed, the turkey was slaughtered.

Now at this point, one may argue that the turkey's error lay in the fact that he did not understand *why* he was fed every day. Our domino example is different. Because we understand that dominos are solid objects with mass, and that momentum is transferred in a collision, we do understand what is happening when the dominos come into contact with each other, and so we can genuinely say that one domino *causes* the next one to fall over. Hume would argue that this is not so. Our laws of physics regarding solid objects and collisions are speculation based on a finite series of observations, so it is absolutely possible that the 'laws' won't always hold and that the results of such experiments will be different in future.

For example, the laws of physics tell us that dominos have their solid form by virtue of the crystalline structure formed by the atoms that make them up and that momentum is transferred by means of the electrostatic Coulomb forces in the outer electrons, which mean that the atoms and molecules of the subsequent domino are repelled when the atoms and molecules of the incoming domino get close enough.

The strength of the repulsion between the electrons is given by Coulomb's law, which states that the repulsive force is inversely related to the square of the distance between them, with a strength proportional to Coulomb's constant.

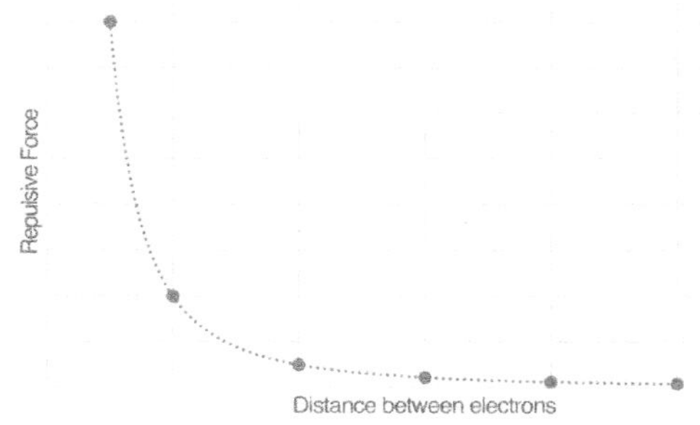

Coulomb's law, showing the strength of the repulsive force between electrons as a function of the distance between them

Coulomb's law has obviously been verified by experiment innumerable times, but let's suppose for simplicity of explanation that the dots on the graph represent the results of the observations made to date. Coulomb's law itself, like all 'laws' of physics, is a hypothesised law of nature, based on speculation after inspecting the observational results[16]. This is a core

[16] Some laws of physics can be said to have been derived from other 'higher' laws of physics and might arguably be said to rest on more solid ground than a law which just describes a relationship between observable variables. However, ultimately these higher laws are themselves the result of induction from observable results.

principle of the scientific method. Scientific laws of nature should be empirical – that is they should be based on observed facts – in order to provide us with the confidence that they are a description of the world around us. If they are not, then this is not science.

So far so good. But who is to say that tomorrow, an experiment will not be done that produces a result reflected by the x on the chart below, that is not consistent with the formula?

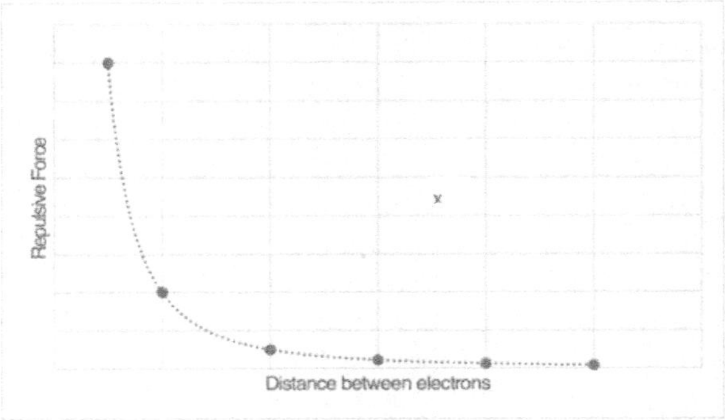

It may well be that the force between electrons is described by a nice smooth curve (indicated by the dotted curve on the graph above) at all points except in a few places where experiments have not been yet conducted. After all, who says that the laws of nature should always be described by simple, smooth, mathematical relationships?

And secondly, who is to say that the value of Coulomb's constant may not change in the future? Physicists nowadays take Coulomb's constant to be 8.988×10^9 Nm^2/C^2 because observations have shown that this is always the case, but isn't this just like the inductivist turkey? Perhaps there will come a time when someone (God?) changes the value of Coulomb's constant for reasons that are opaque to us.

The scientific method takes it as a prerequisite that that the universe is the same for all of us and that the laws of physics don't change. If the laws of physics were subject to change, experiments would not be repeatable and so the laws of nature could not be corroborated. If it turned out that laws of nature *do* change, we would be looking for a higher (unchanging) law describing how the changing laws change. Spontaneous change is a problem, as it means we cannot make predictions (c.f. the Quantum picture presented in chapter 5 – but at least here results are predictable with a sufficient number of trials). So far, science appears to be making progress on the assumption that the laws of physics don't change, but we cannot be certain that this will always be the case.

Science makes progress through a combination of both inductive and deductive reasoning. The scientific hypotheses or laws are inferred through induction and then tested using a deductive approach. If law A is an accurate description of the way the world works, then we should be able to observe phenomenon B. If we then observe something different to phenomenon B, we can conclude that there is something wrong with law A.

One example of this in action was during the cholera epidemic in London in the 19th century. At the time, it was believed that the disease was transmitted through the air and could be identified through a signature 'miasma' (a particularly bad smell). However, when the physician John Snow inspected records showing how cases had spread in a particular part of London, he noticed a pattern suggesting that cases were centred on a particular water pump on Broad Street. He formed an alternative hypothesis that the disease was transmitted through drinking water. He eventually persuaded the authorities to test the hypothesis by removing the handle of the water pump, thereby making the water inaccessible. If the miasma hypothesis was correct, this would have no impact on cholera cases, whereas if the water transmission hypothesis was correct, the action would be expected to result in a reduction in cases. Following the removal of the pump handle, cases reduced dramatically, allowing people to deduce that the miasma hypothesis was incorrect, and corroborating the water transmission hypothesis, thereby furthering our knowledge by improving our understanding of cholera.

Falsificationism

The idea that scientific laws cannot be proven to be true for all future experiments was highlighted by the 20th century philosopher of science, Karl Popper (1902-1994). Popper was born and raised in Vienna in Austria, but spent a significant amount of his career at the University of London, where he was professor of logic and scientific method. He insisted that scientific laws can never be proven to be true, but only be disproven, or 'falsified' as he coined it[xxx]. Experiments that produce results in line with predictions can only be said to support , or 'corroborate' the law, but cannot be said to prove it. There is always the possibility that a future experiment or future observations will show the law to be false. A famous example of this was the orbit of Mercury. Detailed observations of its orbit as far back as 1859 showed that its movement was not in line with that predicted by Newton's laws.

However, some have since argued that it is not even clear that laws *can* be falsified[xxxi]. There are other reasons why experimental results may disagree with predictions other than the law being wrong. Perhaps the problem is with a different part of the theory to the one I think I am testing. If we go back to our simple circuit again, my theory might be that 'the battery has sufficient voltage to light the light'. I connect the battery to the light, but the light does not light. Has this disproved my theory? It may that the battery was not connected properly or other mistakes were made in the running of the experiment. Perhaps the results were deliberately manipulated.

Even so, it seems likely that most people would agree that with enough rigour, these other factors can be controlled so that the theory itself can be tested. Popper says firmly that a theory that cannot be tested does not qualify as a scientific theory. For example, someone might have a theory that the universe is populated by giant invisible insubstantial pink ghost unicorns that stride majestically through the cosmos. They might argue that being invisible, we cannot see them, and being insubstantial, we have no way of detecting them. Unfortunately, as we are unable to interact with them in any way, we are not able to set up any kind of experiment to detect whether they exist or not. We cannot show that this theory is right or wrong, but we can say that it is not a *scientific* theory if it cannot be tested. The second point to make is that irrespective of whether or not the giant ghost unicorns actually exist, we can say that they don't *de facto* exist. This means that as it makes no difference to us whether they exist or not, to all intents and purposes they don't exist in any meaningful way. I will return to this issue later.

If the point of science is to get to the truth of how the universe is structured and how it operates, then things are starting to look bad. We have just seen how we can never be confident that any 'Theory of Everything' that we might come up with is correct – we might perform an experiment at a later date that shows it is wrong. Even if the theory was correct, we would have no way of knowing that it was correct, as we have no way of knowing that it couldn't be falsified in future! This is devastating for anyone who begins the journey of science believing that this is the road to unlocking the secrets of the universe. We just cannot ever know if we have arrived at our destination. But perhaps all is not lost. There are some who have tried to show that although we cannot guarantee ever getting to the truth, we can get closer and closer to it. This idea is known as 'Convergent Realism'.

Instrumentalism and Convergent Realism

Since physicists can never be sure that their theories correctly capture the way nature behaves, it is arguably somewhat strong to call them 'laws' of nature, as that implies that they are somehow sacrosanct, decreed by God and incontestable. Perhaps 'Guidelines of Nature' would be a more accurate description, although some might argue that this label lacks gravitas! Instead, for practical purposes, physicists view their theories as *models* of nature which may or may not be true. Different models are useful for different purposes. Although it is well known that Newton's Laws are not a true description of the way the universe behaves, they are still useful. Newton's equations yield an accurate enough answer for most purposes.

However, by thinking of our laws of nature as a mathematical model, this raises another question. When we build a model, whether it is a physical or a mathematical one, it is always built with a certain aim in mind. A model of an aeroplane might be designed to show what the aeroplane looks like, but might not have all the same moving parts as the actual aeroplane that it is modelling. In financial services, actuaries and analysts regularly build mathematical models of expected future contractual payments, but, depending on what is being investigated, they may not include the full complexity of the contractual obligation.

Instrumentalism

Now what is the purpose of our models of nature, if it is not to find out how nature is actually structured? Some might say that what matters in a model of nature, is not that it faithfully represents the thing that it is a model of, but that it accurately predicts natural phenomena. The model should allow us to predict in advance what will happen in a certain situation, such that we can then test this by experiment. If the model output agrees with experiment, we can go on to apply these models in such fields as engineering and technology and can say we have a better understanding of how nature behaves. Note that this is an understanding of 'how nature behaves' rather than 'how the world is'. As with the model aeroplane discussed above, the model of nature need not be an accurate reflection of how nature actually *is*, as long as it is fit for purpose – as long as its outputs agree with experimental results. As discussed above, it is impossible for us to know whether the models are actually an accurate representation of reality.

Over the centuries, our models of nature have involved a number of weird and wonderful entities, such as atoms, genes, the aether, space-time and photons as wells as different structures such as deterministic/probabilistic, three/four-dimensional and infinite/finite. The entities postulated in our models are not directly observable and we can only inspect them indirectly. That is to say, we can only test whether these entities exist by setting up an experiment which would result in different observable phenomena if they did exist *versus* if they didn't. We saw this when looking at the existence of the aether in chapter six. There was no way of directly observing the aether, but scientists knew that if it did exist, light would travel at a different relative speed in one direction than in the other. Scientists try to get around the fact that these entities are not directly observable by trying to observe their knock-on effects.

But although such an experiment might show that the universe behaves in a way that is *consistent* with a particular entity existing (or not existing, in the case of the aether), it doesn't actually *prove* whether the entity in question exists, as we cannot observe the entity directly. This has led some people to say that our models are no more than instruments for explaining the behaviour of the things that we *can* observe. Terms like 'photon' are just convenient ways of succinctly describing features of the model, but no more than that.

This might explain why we have so much difficulty describing what a photon actually is. Is it a wave? Is it a particle? Once we appreciate that it is no more than an idea, a stepping-stone, that helps us understand the behaviour of real objects, then, one might argue, it is not necessarily surprising that we have trouble conceptualising it in terms of real objects – because it *isn't* a real object. Claims that these entities are real, physical objects cannot be justified and we are being indulgent, over-stepping the mark as it were, by ascribing a real existence to these theoretical entities. This is the approach known as instrumentalism. The opposing view, that there *are* actual physical objects out there to which these terms refer, is called scientific realism.

Under instrumentalism, the atoms that make up our physical world may once have been said to be an example of one of these instruments. The idea that matter is made up of tiny fundamental building blocks dates back at least to the time of the ancient Greeks ('atom' derives from the ancient Greek work 'atomos' than means 'uncuttable') and so well before they could be observed in any way. Instrumentalism might have said that we have no justification for believing that they really exist as physical objects in our world if we cannot observe them. However, time marches on and technology improves and these days, as seen in chapter four, we *can* directly observe atoms with an electron microscope. Presumably this discovery upgrades the ontological status of the atom from 'useful instrument' to 'real object'.

Or does it? As discussed in chapter 4, can we really say that we have observed the atom directly? All we have really observed is a picture on a screen or a piece of paper. On this basis, the atom is still an instrument which allows us to explain the output from the electron microscope. So perhaps even under instrumentalism, the line between which entities qualify as 'real' and which do not is not clear cut. Things are starting to get complicated, and it is perhaps worth asking at this stage whether it is important to make a realist / instrumentalist distinction. While we cannot prove that these objects exist (until perhaps they can in some sense be observed), both scientists and lay people talk about electrons and photons in the sense of them being real physical objects, just as real as the aeroplanes etc that they make up, but on a smaller scale. Perhaps this is because, for a lot of us, the idea that the goal of science is merely to predict the behaviour of phenomena just isn't enough. We don't just want to know what will happen; we want to know how and why things happen that way. Is there not a human drive to not just be able to predict what will happen, but to truly understand it, to understand the make-up of reality and the causes of our experiences?

And so while the existence of such theoretical objects cannot be proven, equally, one might argue that there is nothing to say that they *don't* exist. Even if, in years to come, further work provides a bit more clarity on what a photon actually is, as things stand there is no reason to think that the suggestion that the photon is a physical thing cannot be correct.

Convergent Realism

To put scientific realism on a firmer footing, it has been argued that while we have not yet arrived at a Theory of Everything, we can say that our current theories are 'more true' than older, falsified, theories. That is to say that the entities and structures in our newer models are more like the actual entities and structures in the real world than those postulated in our older theories. And that therefore, in time, we will not only get a better description of how the universe behaves, but that we can, in principle, get to a state where we have good knowledge, pretty much, of how it actually *is*; it's make-up / structure. This assertion is based on the idea that in order to improve the predictive power of a model, it needs to be refined to be a better representation of how the universe actually is. In other words, if my model gives erroneous predictions, this is because it is an over-simplification of how reality is. The more accurate the model, in terms of its representation of underlying reality, the better the predictions and conversely, the better the predictions, the more representative of reality the model must be. This idea, known as 'Convergent Realism' was attacked in a 1981 paper by American philosopher of science Larry Laudan[xxxii].

Laudan highlighted a number of theories which gave good predictions, but which had subsequently turned out to be wrong. His list included the 'phlogiston' model of heat transfer, which saw phlogiston as that part of a substance which is released during the burning process. Under this model, when wood is burned, the phlogiston is released into the air. This explains why the amount of ash left over at the end is much smaller than the amount of wood you start with. The problem with the convergent realism idea can be brought to light when we look at the transition from Newtonian mechanics to Einstein's relativistic mechanics. As we saw in chapter 6, at the macroscopic level, both theories produce broadly the same results (this is known as the correspondence principle – the idea that any new theory should be able to reproduce the successes of the old theory at an appropriate limit). It is only at the scale of the very large where the results diverge materially. However, despite the difference in results being very small for most purposes, conceptually the two theories are very different.

The discrepancies are most notable in their characterisation of the fundamental fabric of the universe – space and time. Recall that in Newton's theory, space is three dimensional and time is separate and the same for all of us. Einstein's General Relativity is set in a curved four-dimensional space-time. However, at the everyday level, the difference this makes to the behaviour of objects is negligible. Might it not be then, that a future theory of the universe, which improves our predictive accuracy only minutely in most cases, could nonetheless show that our current scientific theories are fundamentally wrong in their description of how the universe is structured?

After all, even if we can find a Theory of Everything that survives all our attempts at falsification, who is to say that that the universe could not have a completely different structure to that envisaged by the Theory of Everything? While we might expect a more representative model to give better predictions, the converse that more accurate predictions must mean a more representative model does not follow.

Indeed, bringing this around to the question of God, we could consider the 'Divine Watchmaker' scenario considered in chapter 2. God may set the universe running according to some laws – our identification of these laws will only be a partial description of everything – a description of just the universe, rather than a description of the universe plus God. This is similar to the invisible pink ghost unicorns scenario considered in the last section. We can understand how the world behaves without reference to the ghost unicorns, but, given that they exist, our understanding of how the universe *is* will be incomplete.

At this point, some may suggest that to all intents and purposes, the pink ghost unicorns *don't* exist. If the ghost unicorns are undetectable and have no bearing on our lives, then they may as well be said to not exist – the world would be the same whether they existed or not, so why complicate things? This approach is known as Occam's Razor. If there are two explanations for the same set of facts, Occam's Razor says to cut out the superfluous bits and go for the simplest. However Occam's Razor is a just a *convention*. There is no reason why the simplest explanation must necessarily be the correct one.

In 1982, Hardin and Rosenberg, from the Syracuse University department of philosophy, replied to Laudan's initial paper, saying that it doesn't really matter if we get the details wrong on how these entities are structured. What matters is that when we talk about a photon, we are talking about a physical thing, rather than just an idea. Laudan countered that if you are open to the term photon referring to a whole host of different possible objects, then you are abandoning the core assertion of Realism, that science can get to know the universe as it really is. Laudan characterised this position as 'Realism without the Real'.

To close then, it is worth keeping front of mind that our models are just that – models. They represent reality in terms that are meaningful to us. But as we saw earlier, the world as we see it, is a world generated for us by our brains, which means that reality appears to us through the filter of the human mind. Who is to say that the world as it really is in itself is structured in such a way that is meaningful to us as humans? Our more recent physical theories such as relativity and quantum mechanics are taking us away from our everyday concepts and introducing ideas such as 'curved space' and objects being both a wave and a particle. These ideas are difficult to make sense of. Who is to say that the true nature of the universe can even be understood by us at all?

The scientific method has allowed us to make great progress over the centuries in understanding how the universe behaves. But ultimately, science cannot help us answer the question of whether God exists because it doesn't have the tools to tell us how the universe actually *is*. To make further progress in understanding the true structure of the universe, we will need to move on from the world of science and delve into the world of philosophy.

Chapter 8

8. To Be is to be Perceived?

Now is perhaps a good time to take stock of where our investigations have taken us. We started off with the common-sense picture of reality that we are born into a world of objects, we open our eyes, the world floods in and knowledge of the world results. As we examined this picture more closely, things have started to unravel. Firstly, we noted in chapter 4 that there is much of the world that we cannot perceive. Then we discovered that even the things we do perceive do not necessarily reflect the way the world actually is. And then finally, in the last section, we discovered that it was impossible to obtain knowledge about the way the world really is and even began to suspect that the way the world is may be something that is beyond our capability to understand.

Pythagoras is renowned for saying "All the world is numbers", but perhaps it would be more accurate to say "All the world is models". Our brains conjure up a model of the world for us to live in. Our science produces models of how this world behaves. How do we get beyond the models and get to the facts about the world around us?

In light of all the doubts that have been raised, it is perhaps time to return to first principles and attempt to pin down what we can actually know for certain. At the start of the book, we examined past attempts to establish the existence of God through reason alone and found them wanting. We also established that it won't be possible to establish the existence of God or otherwise through scientific discovery, as the possibility will always remain that the world could be different to how it is represented in our models. How, therefore, should we proceed next? There is a sense that we might be on the wrong track in trying to use scientific methods, as they only provide insights into how features of the physical world interact. And who is to say that God is even part of the physical universe? So the only place left for us is to begin by firmly establishing what we *do* know about reality and proceed from there. This takes us into the realm of philosophy.

The study of what things exist in the world is known as ontology, which is closely related to the broader subject of metaphysics, the study of the nature of these things and how they interact. There is a long history in western philosophy of thinkers attempting to get to grips with this at a fundamental level. Plato conceived of a world of Ideas or Forms which contained idealised version of the objects we encounter in the everyday world, while Empedocles is credited with idea that everything is composed of four roots: the elements earth, air, fire and water, which are brought together through love and driven apart by strife. Later on, philosophers in the 17th century, such as Leibniz, were well aware that our senses can deceive us, and that empirical evidence may not be reliable as a guide to how the universe actually is. For these philosophers, known as Rationalists, the only reliable guide to discovering the truth about reality was to use reason alone. Because what is logically true, is necessarily and always true, only reason and logic can give us truths about the world that are free from doubt. They attempted therefore to come to an understanding of how the universe must be, through an analysis of concepts. For example, it could be argued that any composite object can be divided into its parts, but that at some stage, we must reach the smallest possible building blocks that are combined to make up the universe. Leibniz used this kind of approach to develop his theory of 'monads'. Under this theory, these elementary particles are closely linked to the idea of the soul. Physical matter has a size and anything with a size can be split up, at least in theory, into smaller pieces. On the other hand, the soul is necessarily singular – it makes no sense to talk about half a soul. The idea that everything in the universe is imbued with some kind of soul may appear quite outlandish today, but the Rationalists viewed their theories as much more than romantic speculation – they were the inevitable result of the ironclad forces of logic.

However, a deductive logical truth is only as good as the premises upon which it is based. Where do the premises of Rationalist metaphysics come from? We are told that they are grounded on 'self-evident' truths, that no sane person would deny, but the fact that there have been many different such rationalist ontologies leaves the Rationalist position open to the charge of being dogmatic and arbitrary. And this was exactly the accusation made by Hume when he railed that every volume of school metaphysics we should commit to the flames, for it can contain "nothing but sophistry and illusion".

Scepticism and Idealism

So where do we go from here? If we can't rely on either our experiences *or* our reason to tell us about the world, what can we rely on? In philosophy, the approach of starting with what you, as an individual, know for sure, and building from there is known as the 'critical method'. This approach could perhaps be said to have started with 17th Century philosopher René Descartes (1596-1650) and his famous maxim 'I think, therefore I am'. Descartes noted that everything you are seeing and feeling, like the book or screen in front of you right now, could just be a dream or a hallucination. It could have all been cooked up for you by an evil demon and might not actually exist in reality. The only thing I can know for certain, says Descartes, is that I am thinking *something*. Therefore the only thing that I can be sure actually exists in the real world is me. Everything else might be an illusion.

This idea that reality, or reality as humans can know it, is fundamentally mental, mentally constructed or otherwise immaterial is known as idealism, and it can take a number of different forms. A common idea is that the world 'outside' could be very different to the world that we actually experience. As we saw in chapter 4, all the information we receive about the outside world arrives through our senses. This is then translated into a picture of reality by our brains, to form the world we actually experience. So who is to say that the picture conjured up by our brains is a true representation of the outside world? Descartes' evil demon concept is updated in the classic 1999 Wachowski brothers film 'The Matrix', where people have the impression they are living their normal lives, but in reality are plugged into a machine, with their brains stimulated artificially. Could this nightmare scenario actually be true? All of our experience of the outside world comes to us through our senses, which send signals to our brains – if our eyes received blue light, the signal sent to our brains is different to that which is sent if our eyes experience red light. But if your brain received the red light signal artificially, how would you ever know the difference?

The theory that certain knowledge is impossible is known as *scepticism* and there is a long and proud tradition of such doubters in Western philosophy. The next important contributor to this line of thinking was the Scottish philosopher David Hume. Hume claimed that as all knowledge comes to us through our senses, we have no reason to believe that everyday concepts that we take for granted, like causation and substance are real. We might think that the strong wind causes the tree to fall over, but all that has happened, is that we have observed a series of correlations. Every time the wind has been strong enough, the tree has fallen over. It has been *blown* over – the faith in causation has worked its way into our language.

Kant

In the worlds before Monkey, primal chaos reigned.
Tatagatha Buddha, the father Buddha said "With our thoughts, we make the world."

Following the attacks by Descartes and Hume, the common-sense picture of reality by this point lay in tatters and there was a desperate need for a picture of reality that was built on more solid foundations. Perhaps the philosopher who made the most progress with this project was the 18th century German philosopher Immanuel Kant (1724-1804), who famously stated that it was the sceptical challenge laid down by Hume that rose him from his 'dogmatic slumbers' and forced him to confront it head on. After all, even though we have no reason to believe that the common-sense picture is true, we still rely on it every day. We act and behave as if there really are solid objects out there, obeying causal laws, and this approach works well. Why does it work well if its grounds are so questionable?

Central to Kant's project was to find a solution to the problem of reality, namely how do objects in the world become known to us and cause images in our minds?[xxxiii] Or as Kant puts it in his 1772 letter to a fellow German philosopher and physician Markus Herz, "What is the ground of the relation of that in us which we call 'representation' to the object?". By 'representation', Kant is talking about our own sense impressions – the aeroplane as it appears to us. Now under the common-sense picture, this is easily answered. The world out there gives off information which is picked up by our senses to create images in our minds. But for Kant, this is a complete non-answer and begs the question[17]. It's like answering the question of 'how does a microscope work?' by saying 'By magnifying the image'. The question is then 'Yes, but *how* does it magnify the image?' Okay, so we pick up on information given off by the world. But how is it that we are capable of making use of the information given off by the world? This is the question Kant is trying to answer. Might there not also be ghost unicorns out there that we don't perceive, because we are not capable of any kind of interaction with them? Perhaps one could answer that the reason we don't perceive the ghost unicorns (if they exist) is because of evolution. We don't need to be able to detect the ghost unicorns because they don't affect us. We have evolved to pick up only the information that matters. But this still doesn't explain how it is done. Kant is asking how it is that the image we see in our minds actually represents anything that is 'out there'.

Kant can be seen as building on the work done by Descartes. Descartes asked 'What can I know for certain?' and concluded that although everything he experienced could be a dream, at least he could know that

[17] Begging the question is when you assume in your proof, the very thing you are trying to prove.

he existed. Kant said, okay, so everything I experience might not be real, but my experience does have certain features. For example, my experiences change and I am able to experience several different things at any one instant. It is not the case, for example, that my experience is just blackness. Kant then asked, 'what must be true in order for my experience to have these features?' This approach is sometimes known as the 'Critical Method'.

Kant noted that one of the features of our experience is that things change. You could imagine some hypothetical creature whose experience is fixed. That creature would have no concept of time. Put in that context, time can be considered to be the aspect of our faculty to perceive the world which facilitates changes in our experiences. Furthermore, another feature of our experience is that it has contrast. We do not, for example, experience a point of blackness, followed by a point of redness and so on. A creature with that experience would have no concept of space. Put in that context, space can be considered to be the aspect of our faculty to perceive the world which facilitates contrast in our experience at a given moment in time.

It is important to understand that for Kant, whether space and time are features of the world itself is a secondary question. Even if the world itself existed in space and time, this does not necessarily mean that we would have the ability to experience it. The universe may exist in ten or more dimensions; yet we can only perceive three. Instead, for Kant, space and time are primarily the means by which we experience the universe. Kant called them 'modes of intuition' and saw them as fundamental features of our make-up, rather than properties of the universe. Remember we are starting from the point of our self-consciousness only – we are considering the brute facts of our experience. The approach is not concerned with speculating on the drivers of this in the real world.

Kant's ideas on time are consistent with the idea of time discussed in chapter 6, where we talked about measuring time by the repetitive occurrences of observable phenomena, such as the rotation of the earth (1 day) or the frequency of vibrations of a quartz crystal. By making time a feature of your experience, rather than a property of the universe in general, Kant leaves it open as to whether you have experienced the same number of seconds as me[xxxiv]. Or to put it another way, he leaves it open as to whether yours and my identical quartz crystals have vibrated the same number of times. They must have if they are identical, right? This is the philosophical error Newton made in assuming that there is some kind of 'background time' part of the universe dictating the progression of all things. As Newton put it

> *"Absolute true and mathematical time, of itself and by its own true nature flows uniformly on, without regard to anything external".*

Certainly, we might say that Newton started out with the best of intentions. Following the scientific spirit of being guided only by experimental evidence, he stated in a preface to his dynamical theory that he would forego abstract speculation and deal only with observable facts. It was Ernst Mach that pointed out that if he were to deal only with observable facts, he needed to deal with things you can observe like the repetitive motion of physical systems i.e. clocks. This concept of time without clocks is abstract speculation and so is not justified. We saw in chapter 6 how this metaphysical notion of universal background space and time, that is the same for all of us, was later shown to be wrong.

Similar considerations apply to space. We experience the world existing in three dimensions, and under the common-sense picture, this is because this is the way the world is. We see it as it is, with some aspects filtered out if our senses are not capable of detecting them. It was only when Einstein's theory of relativity came along, describing the universe in terms of a curved four-dimensional space-time, that the idea that the way we see the world may be very different to the way it actually is took hold. However in a sense, Kant anticipated this over a hundred years before Einstein came along. Under Kant's philosophy, space is an 'outer-sense' – that part of our make-up that allows us to experience different things simultaneously, rather than being an intrinsic feature of the universe.

It is important to understand that for Kant, space and time are not *part* of our experiences because without space and time, there could not *be* experiences as we know them. Space and time are vehicles for our experiences. We could perhaps contrast the world as we see it with a PacMan game, which interprets incoming data signals as events taking place in a two-dimensional space. The two-dimensional space provides the setting for events to be experienced, but is not the source of the experience. Or instead, we could perhaps imagine an alien species that experiences reality differently to us. Perhaps they see it in a fixed ten-dimensional space – such creatures would have no concept of time or change. Kant would say we have no grounds for believing that the concepts of space and time have meaning outside our experience – that the concept of something being 'over there' only has meaning in the framework of how *we* experience reality, but there are no grounds for believing that reality is intrinsically spatial or temporal in itself. In this framework, our scientific theories, which are cast in spatial and temporal terms, become theories of how our experiences change, rather than theories of the behaviour of any 'outside world'.

Kant also builds on the work of Descartes by considering more carefully what is meant by the concept of 'I' or the self. Under the common-sense picture, 'I' is used to distinguish between me and the other objects in the world, whether this be in terms of my body (e.g. 'something hit me') or my consciousness (e.g. I moved my finger). But under the idealist picture, it is not so clear what 'I' refers to. If everything that makes up the world around me is a construct of my imagination, then is not everything part of the all-consuming 'me'? The dream, the world and my imagination are all one and the same thing. In a dream you can wake up, and get back to the real world of concrete objects, whereas for Descartes it could be that the dream is all there is. So what is there that is *not* part of 'me' in this case?

This has led some commentators to claim that Descartes overreached himself even with the extremely limited knowledge claim that 'I' exist in any meaningful way. They point out that in order for there to be an 'I', there must be something else that is not 'I', and that this is yet to be established. Descartes is considering the question of what he can know to be real. This question involves three separate concepts: the self (the 'I'), one's experiences (the things that may or may not be real) and the real world (the set of things that are indeed real). Descartes says all my other experiences may not be part of the real world, but at least I can know that *I* am. But Descartes is getting ahead of himself! The idealist will say all I really know for sure is that I am having experiences – this idea of a 'real world' is a third thing, a metaphysical concept, and we have no justification for believing that it even exists. Therefore it doesn't make much sense to claim I am an object within it. Furthermore, it is not clear what we mean by *I,* whether I am justified as viewing myself as separate from my experiences. All Descartes has shown, under this line of reasoning, is that I can be aware of my present mental states; that there is thinking going on.

It feels, though, as if we *should* be able to get to a more satisfactory answer and here again Kant comes along to help. He starts by asking whether we can say that there is anything that isn't 'me'. To answer this question, Kant takes a close look at what it means to be self-conscious, focusing in on Descartes' point that an 'I think' can accompany each of our sense impressions. We might imagine a less-sophisticated life-form that has a form of consciousness, but is not self-conscious. This lifeform might feel pain when it comes into contact with boiling water and perhaps it has evolved to recoil by some reflex action. But this life-form doesn't *think*. It doesn't make a decision to move away – every movement is an automated reaction[18]. The question we can ask is 'could such a creature be said to have a sense of self, separate from its experiences?' Kant maintains that if I am unable to think about my sensations, then the notion that there is an *I* standing in relation to my experiences disappears. This assertion might remind us of a number of eastern religions that teach that if you are able to stop actively thinking, through meditation perhaps, then the boundary between you and the rest of the universe disappears – you become one with reality. Conversely, says Kant, if I can think about my sensations, then there must be something, an object, that I am thinking about. If I am thinking about the book in front of me, this is more than

[18] Of course it could be argued that your thoughts are also automated reactions! We will explore this further when we consider Free Will in chapter 14.

just passive awareness of the texture and colours of the pages. I am actively thinking about the book as a distinct object; something that is ontologically separate from me.

This is a big advance. Kant notes that thinking would not be possible if there were not things to think about and so Kant has established that other objects exist, just as surely as I exist. We don't know in what form they exist yet – we are certainly not at the stage where we can say that they exist in the 'real world'. But then again, we can't say that *we* exist in the real world either. But we *have* established that other objects are just as real as I am. Kant calls these objects 'transcendental objects', because they 'transcend' sense experience. The transcendental object is related to our sense impressions, in that it gives the sense impressions something to attach to, but the transcendental object is separate from our sense impressions – it is not just another word for our sense impressions. We know this, because we can compare our situation of self-conscious experience with our lower life form that is unable to think. That life form just reacts automatically to sense impressions, but does not consider objects. It is the fact that we can think that means these transcendental objects necessarily exist for us. We think and therefore we have objects which give us something to think about. Note that at the moment the nature of these transcendental objects is unknown. We have not yet even considered whether they exist 'in reality', 'out there', for what is 'out there', when space is nothing more than a mode of intuition? All we have done at the moment is establish that it makes sense to consider myself as having experience of objects, the nature of which are still to be decided.

Even though we haven't yet even established the existence of the real world, we are making progress. From the start of this book, up to now, all we have been doing is knocking down everything we thought we knew about the world. Kant here is actually building something up. He has shown that the human self-conscious experience necessarily involves objects existing in space and time. Next Kant goes on to consider what else must be true for an object to exist in space and time.

Firstly, says Kant, in order for us to be able to think about objects, they must have continuity through time, despite any changes they may undergo. We don't just see a kaleidoscope of changing colours, so when we think about an object over a period of time, it must have some characteristic that means it remains the same object throughout. This is the concept of *substance*. The object may move about. We may look at it from a different angle. It may change colour or shape, but its substance, that which lies behind these changing perceptions, is the same. We are now in a position to answer Hume's challenge from chapter 4 – what is the aeroplane *apart* from its colour, shape and texture etc? The aeroplane is the transcendental object which gives it its identity. Its substance remains constant while other qualities shift, allowing the object to maintain its identity as time passes. The question this raises however, is how is it possible that we are able to understand the changes that we experience as changes in the object itself, rather than just changes in our perception of it?

Kant illustrates the difference here by considering two scenarios. The first looks at the point of view of a subject walking around a house. As the subject moves, their perceptions change – different parts of the house come into view. But the house itself is not changing. This is contrasted with a boat moving downstream while the subject observes from the riverbank. In this scenario, the subject's perceptions change, just like in the first scenario, as the boat moves past successive features of the riverbank. But here it is not only the subject's perception that is changing. The boat is also changing its position with respect to the riverbank.

Because Kant's objects are separate from our representations of them, we need something that facilitates change in objects; some reason to view objects as themselves changing – to view the boat as moving down the river rather it just being the case that we are just looking differently at a static situation. Now what is the difference between the two scenarios that means we are experiencing objects changing in the second, but not in the first? In the first scenario, changes in our perceptions are a result of our own agency. If we choose to walk around the house in one direction, we will experience it differently to how we would if we walked around it in a different direction. However, in the riverboat scenario, the change happens irrespective of our view on it. Kant notes that in the second scenario, the change is necessary and irreversible. It is necessary in the sense that the boat moving down the river is not influenced by how we view it and irreversible in the sense that retracing our positioning will not move the boat back upstream.

Now we already have an everyday term for changes that are necessary and irreversible, and that is to say that they are *caused.* Note that we are not talking here about some *external source* of the change in the objects – remember these are not physical objects, but just objects in the abstract sense of being separate from the subject. Kant is talking about the necessary change in the object's configuration that is required to maintain its role in our conceptual scheme. Because this change is necessary and irreversible, it fits the definition of a caused change. The first boat colliding with a second boat will necessarily result in it the second boat colliding with an adjacent third boat, as the objects change configuration to fit our conceptual scheme. Or in other words, the first collision causes the second collision. Note that importantly, causation is about the relation of objects of our experience to each other. It has nothing to do with how the objects of our experience relate to any 'real world'.

In summary then, according to Kant, in order for me to be able to think, there must be objects for me to think about. And in order for these objects to make sense to me, they must exist in space and time, be formed of substances and interact with each other causally, just like the common-sense picture. The common-sense picture is true therefore, insofar as it correctly describes the world we experience. Kant claims to have vindicated the common-sense picture of the world around us and successfully defended it from the sceptical attacks of Descartes and Hume. But at what cost?

Chapter 9

9. A Copernican Revolution

When discussing Descartes, we spoke about three things – reality, our *experience* of reality and ourselves. But how does Kant deal with this philosophical triumvirate? So far in our discussion, we have only covered the last two – ourselves and our experiences. We've seen how Kant thinks our experience of reality must be, if we are self-conscious. However, he hasn't even touched on what this implies for the nature of reality itself. Perhaps unsurprisingly, Kant's view is that knowledge of how reality is constituted *independently* of the human perspective is impossible. So far we have used a variety of terms for this, like the 'real world', the 'outside world' etc. But Kant has shown that while the world of our *experience* is spatial, this doesn't necessarily mean that an 'outside world' exists in the sense just described. So from now on, we are going to need to be a little more precise with our terminology. For a start, I'll use 'Independent Reality' to refer to the world or universe, as it exists in itself, independently of the human perspective[19].

How can we begin to get a handle on what Independent Reality is like? At this point, we might recall that within Kant's metaphysics, objects of our experience are constructed by our minds as focal points for incoming

[19] Some commentators use the term 'objective' reality, but this can lead to confusion between it meaning a world that is not subjective and it meaning a world of objects (which could still be a subjective world).

sensory data, and so the *form* of these objects depends on our make-up as human beings. If we consider again the perspective of our ten dimensional timeless alien, the form of their objects will be very different to ours. And therefore it is not clear what form any independently real object might take, nor how they relate to our objects of experience. The objects we experience are, if you like, the brain's model of reality, just like we saw in chapter four with the rubber hand experiment – with the mind constructing an object to fit the incoming data. Kant concludes that we cannot know anything about these independently real objects. Our knowledge of reality is restricted to knowledge of our point of view.

So where does that leave us? Must we admit defeat and accept that the nature of independent reality will forever remain a mystery? Kant would say that on the contrary, he has reached the destination and discovered everything that there is to discover about the nature of reality. Humans see things in spacio-temporal terms. It makes no sense to ask what the 'real' form of objects is because the only form that we can make sense of is the spacio-temporal form. Kant's point is that although people like Hume are right to say you can't know anything about objects, other than in respect of how you perceive them, this is no problem. It is only our experience that has any reality for us, not some behind-the-scenes objects, as they are constituted from outside our perspective. The objects as they are in themselves, are irrelevant. We are reminded of the situation with the ghost unicorns – they may exist as a thought provoking curiosity, but they have no bearing on our lives. It is only the objects of our experience that we interact with, can model scientifically and that give the world meaning. Kant therefore dismisses Hume's worries about ghost unicorns.

Kant's project involved what he called a 'Copernican Revolution' in the relationship between the subject and the object. Or, as he puts it, it is the representation that makes the object possible rather than the object that makes the representation possible. In the early 16th century, Nicholas Copernicus revolutionised our thinking about our place in the universe by re-introducing the idea from ancient philosophy that our astronomical observations could be better explained by considering the earth as orbiting the sun, rather than vice versa. Kant proposes an analogous reversal in our thinking about the subject-object relation. The common-sense picture says we picture objects in our minds, based on how they are. Kant says

> *'Hitherto it has been assumed that all our knowledge must conform to objects'* whereas instead we *'must therefore make trial whether we might not have more success in the task of metaphysics, if we suppose that objects must conform to our knowledge'.*

This reversal only makes sense if the concept of an 'object' is understood differently in each case[20]. The common-sense picture sees an object as something with a form of its own, independent of how it is perceived (an 'objective object', if you will). For Kant, the object is an object of our experience, an object as constructed by our minds. It therefore has a subjective element (a 'subjective object'). Therefore, the price Kant pays for validating the common-sense picture of reality is that it is only true at the level of human experience. Reality, as constructed outside of human perception is left as something that cannot be known.

*

Thus, although Kant aims to defend a common-sense picture at the everyday level, ultimately it is an idealism. This might make some people uneasy. If the world I live in is a mental construct, then I don't know what's really out there and this is a threat. With that in mind, let's spend a few paragraphs exploring some of the implications of Kant's idealism.

As a mentally constructed reality, idealism is often likened to a dream. So, what is the difference between a dream and the real world? Well a dream is something you wake up from. Okay, so what is the difference between the real world and a dream that you never wake up from? We can say that a dream is a figment of your imagination, whereas the real world actually exists. But what does it mean to say that the real world 'actually exists'? One thought might be that when you die the dream ends, whereas the real

---

[20] Kant is not claiming that we can affect independently real objects with our minds, using Uri Geller like spoon bending powers.

world carries on. At least in the minds of other people. Another distinction between dreams and the real world could be their source. You are the source of your dreams, so dreams are always recast versions of things you have seen before. They lack to potential to introduce anything genuinely new. Whereas the source of real life experiences lies outside you. Idealisms are sometimes challenged on the grounds that if the world is primarily a mental construct, it can be whatever you like. But note that under Kant's transcendental idealism, although the *form* of our reality is based on our humanity, the *content* still comes from an independent reality. This is right in line with the latest thinking from modern neuroscience, which says that the brain constructs a model of reality based on the incoming data signals.

However, perhaps a more serious objection to idealism might arise when considering the implications for the concept of time. If, as Kant insists, time is not a property of independent reality, this raises some puzzling questions. For example, 'What happens after I die?' We saw that Kant's metaphysics describes how experiences must appear to us, but was silent on the nature of independent reality. This might lead us to ask whether there even is such a thing. The denial that there is anything other than oneself and one's experiences is called Solipsism, and we'll discuss this rather extreme position later. For now, we can say for the Solipsist, when they die, that is the end of everything and so also the end of time. But what about under the Kantian picture, where time is a vehicle for your experience?

Before I was born, I had no experiences and so on Kant's account, there was no time. Yet it can plainly be seen that before other people are born, time is marching on regardless. Does this suggest that time must be a property of the universe after all, as well as being a vehicle for our experience? The key point to understand is that when other people are born, time begins for them, but time was still passing *for me*. I was still alive. I was still experiencing. We are used to describing situations objectively, but under the Kantian picture of the universe, no objective description is possible. There is no disembodied camera from a documentary recording the development of the universe in the absence of any observer.

So let's ask instead 'what happened before *anyone* was alive to observe it?'. If there were no people, there was no time anywhere. Again, it is key to remember that as questions involving 'before' are about time, they are questions about the universe as experienced by us, not about the universe as it is in itself. This needs a bit more unpacking. The empirical evidence tells a story of a universe that developed for 13.8 billion years before any humans were around. Is Kant saying that this doesn't make sense, because before humans, there was no time? No. We need to understand that these are two different ways of looking at the same thing, like a photon that is sometimes best considered as a wave and at other times better considered as a particle. Or that picture which could be a candlestick or could be two faces looking at each other.

The human perspective is a perspective on the universe. When did the universe, as it exists for me, begin? Was it 13.8 billion years ago? Or when I was born, since it obviously couldn't exist for me before I was born? We need to be precise with our phrasing. I started experiencing the universe at the point I was born[21]. The form of this experience was, and is, of a universe that started 13.8 billion years ago. This is the way that I experience the universe – by means of objects that exist in space and time. For me, objects were around before I was born and will continue after I die.

But to ask 'what did the universe look like before there was anyone to observe it' is a muddy question. It is ambiguous. We either mean 'From our perspective now, what did the universe look like before there was anyone to observe it?', in which case the answer is that it spent 13.8 billion

[21] Or perhaps more precisely, when I became conscious

years expanding rapidly with galaxies, stars and planets all forming and dying' or we mean 'Objectively, from a perspectiveless perspective, what is the structure of the universe?' Note, we cannot ask for the perspectiveless structure at a specific point in time, because time implies a human perspective. And the answer here is that this cannot be known because structure implies concepts which implies language with implies a consciousness which implies a perspective. It is the human perspective that allows us to make sense of an otherwise incomprehensible universe. Or so Kant would argue. We are again reminded of the quantum measurement problem or Bishop Berkeley's tree in the quad. The universe may exist in some sense without us, but it is only as observed by us that its objects can have a meaningful form.

We are now perhaps in a better position to address the questions raised in the Cosmological Argument in chapter two, about whether the universe must be the result of a 'first cause'. The concept of causation inherently doesn't have a beginning – we can always continue asking "yes, but what happened before *that*?" or "what caused *that*?". And so the whole concept of a 'first cause' or the 'beginning of time' makes no sense. But if causation is the means by which we understand the world around us, rather than an inherent features of reality, then it does not seem unreasonable to suggest that there are some instances when trying to apply this concept doesn't work. It may work well as a way of understanding our everyday experiences, but perhaps it breaks down when extrapolated back beyond the big bang.

Trendelenburg's Alternative and the Ontological Denial

Many philosophers of science are resistant to the idea that we cannot have knowledge of things as they are in themselves. Scientific realists maintain that the objects posited in our scientific theories, such as atoms and genes are not just abstract concepts from our scientific models, but do correspond to actual objects in independent reality. If it turns out that later experiments show that these objects don't actually exist, then this is just a minor hiccup. Scientists can correct their theories so that they feature the true objects of independent reality. The key point for the scientific realist is that the universe is structured in a certain way, independently of any observer and that our scientific theories can in principle describe it, even if there are a few mistakes along the way before they are described accurately. Kant, on the other hand, would say that our scientific theories only describe the behaviour of objects as they appear to us. The idea that they describe things as they are in themselves is dogmatic. Such an assertion is based on no more than faith.

The idea that concepts such as space, time and substance could be features of the real world, *as well as* being features of human cognition is known as 'Trendelenburg's Alternative' and was first associated with the German philosopher and philologist Adolf Trendelenburg. He argued in 1862 that:

> *"even if we concede the argument that space and time are demonstrated to be subjective conditions which, in us, precede perception and experience, there is still no word of proof to show that they cannot at the same time be objective forms."*

Trendelenburg's idea is that we can accept that concepts such as space, time and substance are features of our cognition. We can also accept that it is impossible to have certain knowledge about the make-up of 'the world outside'. Yet, even given all this, who is to say that the world is not like how we think it is? None of what we have covered so far rules out the possibility that space and time are intrinsic components of the world outside.

This has echoes of the pursuits in physics, covered in the last chapter. We are trying to refine our mathematic models until we get a perfect description of how the universe actually works. If we get there, we won't know it, but the idea is that we could, in theory, get there. However, Trendelenburg's Alternative is *not* the same as scientific realism. The scientific realist recognises the way the universe really is, as the cause of our experiences and therefore hopes to be able to get to how the universe really is, in order to therefore understand our experiences. Kant dashes this hope by saying that whenever you think you are saying something about the nature of the real world, all you are really doing is saying something about the nature of experience. The realist says 'I can understand the real aeroplane in itself as some configuration of different types of atom, which cause the aeroplane that I experience, through their interaction with light etc'. Kant says I'm very happy for you to say that the atomic configuration causes the aeroplane you experience. But those atoms are also objects of experience, albeit at perhaps a deeper level. Remember causation is a concept humans use to make sense of the interactions between objects of experience. Those atoms exist in space and time and are all part of understanding the nature of our experience. With this move, Kant brings what you thought were the building blocks of Independent Reality into the world of experience, and at the same time pushes the true underlying objects of Independent Reality back out of reach. So whether or not Trendelenburg is right in claiming that underlying reality could exist as a structure that is meaningful to us, it is ultimately irrelevant, because unlike with scientific realism, it is not the underlying structure of these things that determines how we conceive of them in experience. Instead, it is our make up as humans that determines that we conceive of them in space and time as causally interacting substances.

Kant himself, denied Trendelenburg's Alternative and claimed that on the contrary, it is impossible even in principle, for space and time to be an aspect of independent reality. If 'space' and 'time' are defined as ways of experiencing – Kant calls them 'modes of intuition' – then it doesn't even make sense to ask if these concepts can be applied to a situation where there is no consciousness around to do any experiencing. Kant argues that even *the idea* of knowledge of things in themselves – things as they are constituted independently of how they are perceived – makes no sense. After all, 'knowledge' implies an understanding and so a point of view, whereas the concept of a 'thing as it is in itself' is a thing in the absence of any particular perspective on it. This position is sometimes known as Kant's Ontological Denial.

An interlocuter may perhaps try to get around the focus on *knowledge* about things in themselves, by asking 'what are the *facts* about things in themselves?' After all, facts are either true or false; they are objective and independent of any particular perspective. However some may still view this as problematic. A fact is either true or false and so must be expressed at a statement. A statement is expressed using some kind of language and involves certain concepts. For example, suppose we wanted to ask perhaps the most basic question about things as they are in themselves, which could be 'Is there more than one?' Is there one thing, that we see as a horse, for example, and a different thing that we see as a cat? Or perhaps one thing that we experience as a photon and a different thing that we experience as a Higgs boson? Or is the thing as it is in itself just one big continuous soup that we experience as a number of changing objects? Even asking this question involves the concept of division – the idea that independent reality has a structure of discrete objects. Kant might argue that this concept only makes sense to us because of our intuition of space, which permits this kind of contrast, and so the idea that independent reality has a structure only makes sense from a human perspective. Any structure is an abstraction. A structure is an intellectual idea that we apply to our experience in order to make sense of it, so it is wrong-headed to imagine that an abstract intellectual construction is inherent in independent reality.

Is this convincing? At this point, you might just point again to Trendelenburg's Alternative. Just because humans are capable of conceptualising abstract structures doesn't mean that Independent Reality cannot itself have a structure. And if it has a structure, who is to say that this structure cannot be grasped by the human intellect? Therefore in this view, the Ontological Denial is not provable. We can also turn Kant's arguments back against him and point out that to claim that Independent Reality is not even in theory comprehensible is to make a knowledge claim about the outside world. In other words, the Ontological Denial is equivalent to a claim that its structure is at a level of complexity that is beyond the comprehension of human cognition. And of course, by Kant's own theory, such knowledge claims about Independent Reality are impossible.

*

So where does all this take us? We have seen that all of our thoughts, knowledge and understanding are shaped by our humanity and so it is impossible to step outside our perspective and get a handle on things as they are objectively, in the absence of any subjective element. If it so happened that independent reality does have features that are in line with the features of our cognition, rather than say, the features of the timeless ten dimensional alien's cognition, this would be a coincidence and we could never know it.

In the decades after the publication of Kant's *Critique of Pure Reason*, the Kantian picture of reality gradually fell out of fashion. This was perhaps more to do with difficulties in accepting some of its consequences than any major flaws in its reasoning – the greatest criticism levelled at Kant's reasoning was against his insistence that we can have knowledge about the world that does not come to us through our senses, which he called '*a priori*' knowledge. The *a priori* knowledge claims in Kant's system include the claim that we experience a world of causally interacting substances – as Hume pointed out, evidence for this does not come through our senses. A denial that such knowledge is possible would reduce Kant's system to a useful model rather than a demonstrable truth. The examples that Kant gives to support his claim of the possibility of *a priori* knowledge have since been undermined[22] and from a 21st Century perspective, it is perhaps fair to say that while modern philosophers view Kant's insights as one of the major achievements of Western philosophy, a Kantian, idealistic outlook is not mainstream among philosophers today, even as a model, and has largely fallen from view of the wider public.

Solipsism

Kant's analysis of experience suggests that independent reality is forever unknowable for us. But this then raises the spectre of solipsism[23], for who is to say that an independent reality even exists at all? Could it be that

---

[22] These include an appeal to the truth of the geometry of Newtonian physics as a description of the world as we can know it, which, as we saw in Section 5 was undermined by Einstein's Relativity.
[23] The word solipsism derives from the latin 'solus' – 'ipse' meaning 'only self'.

these experiences 'just happen'? We are again reminded of Wittgenstein's assertion that a nothing will serve just as well as a something about which nothing could be said. This point was made in a review of Kant's work in the year after it was published. Kant insisted that an independent reality is required in his metaphysics because while the form of appearance derives from the subject (e.g. it being spatio-temporal etc), the content does not. Independent reality is required in order for the objects of our experience to exist – experience must be experience *of* something and therefore appearances must be grounded in an independent reality. However, critics may then question the nature of this grounding. Kant has claimed that causal relations are between objects of experience, but what is this grounding in independent reality if not a causal relation? If we cannot know anything about independent reality, then there is no meaningful mapping between the objects of independent reality and the objects of experience. And if *this* is the case, then the claim that they must have any 'grounding' in independent reality seems empty. For reasons such as this, some critics have argued that this claim is just an assertion, and that Kant's defence of this claim it is not persuasive.

Solipsism is the view that only the self exists. This means that all the objects of your experience are just part of the greater you[24]. They are figments of your imagination and have no independent existence of their own. If you were to die or otherwise be removed from existence, there would be nothing remaining. One of the obvious consequences of this, is that there are no other real people either. Under Solipsism, the people that you interact with are not real people with minds of their own – it would be more accurate to think of them as automatons or zombies, or perhaps like characters in a dream. This question of whether other people really exist is usually put as the 'Problem of Other Minds'. It is intrinsically tied up with the idea of Solipsism and is the subject of much philosophical thought and debate.

We'll explore some of the implications of Solipsism in Part II, but for now it is worth noting that we do not tend to come across people who seriously

[24] We already saw above Kant's argument that there must be objects other than 'you' in order to give you something to think about. But such objects depend on the subject for their existence and so can be thought of as part of 'you' in a wider sense.

accept a solipsistic position; it is more taken as an intellectual exercise to illustrate a particularly extreme form of idealism. Indeed, some philosophers argue that the Solipsist position is incoherent[xxxv]. I will be arguing that the question of whether there is a reality that exits independently of the subject is badly formed, and that the problem of other minds is also ill-conceived.

Arguments that Knock Down Towers

I started the previous chapter by asking what philosophy can tell us about the world around us and how we can make sense of our experiences. And now it seems that we have ended up with essentially three possibilities for the circumstances that lead to the experiences that we have – an independent reality that is intelligible in principle (Trendelenburg's Alternative), an independent reality that is not intelligible (Kant's Ontological Denial) or no independent reality at all (Solipsism). However in all three of these possibilities, the structure of our experience – the fact that it involves causally interacting substances that exist in space and time – is a result of the human condition and this therefore precluded us from be able to infer anything about the structure of this independent reality (if it exists at all).

This lent support for the case against convergent realism – the vain hope that science gradually gets closer to understanding how independent reality is actually structured. Perhaps the common perception of science is that it starts from the position that there is an independent reality that needs modelling. However I would argue that saying this is getting ahead of ourselves. It is our *experiences* that need modelling and the hypothesis that there is an independent reality is part of that model.

Today's common-sense picture of the world could be said to be built on two pillars: those of scientific laws and empirical evidence. We disregard speculation regarding the nature of the world that does not rest on one of these pillars. For example, claims based on concepts such as fate and destiny are treated with scepticism, and reliance is placed on the evidence of our senses over the word of others – "I'll believe it when I see it" being a familiar refrain. But how much reliance can we place on these foundations that support our knowledge of the world?

The pillar of scientific laws, we saw in chapter 7, is built on the pillar of empirical evidence. Under the scientific method, scientific laws are accepted or rejected based on the outcome of experiment – the sole arbiter of a law's truth or falsity. Individual scientists may prefer certain laws based on their elegance and simplicity or based on a certain 'gut feel' about how they understand the universe to be. 'God does not play dice' said Albert Einstein, when considering the new laws of quantum mechanics, and a considerable amount of effort has been expended in producing a model of the sub-atomic world that preserves a form of determinism – the idea that the state of affairs today is determined (caused) by the events of the past with no random element. However, despite these efforts, the laws of quantum mechanics continue to dominate because they best explain the data. Ultimately scientific laws live or die by their agreement with the empirical evidence.

However, we also saw that the pillar of empirical evidence is built on the pillar of scientific laws. When we move a golf ball into our blind spot, our brain tells us that the ball has disappeared, but we don't really believe this. And when we focus on the spot in the middle of Troxler's fading, we do not really believe that the outer circle disappears. We have our scientific understanding of the world, which tells us that the golf ball is still there; it is just that our eyes cannot detect it because the incoming light reflected off the golf ball is hitting our optic nerve, rather than the receptors in our retina. When we focus on the spot in Troxler's fading, our scientific theories tell us that it is not that the outer circle disappears, it is that the brain is discarding the less relevant information.

So we trust the evidence of our senses to the extent that it agrees with our scientific laws. And we trust our scientific laws to the extent that they agree with the evidence of our senses. Neither of the two towers are grounded on the true make-up of the world, rather, each of the two towers is grounded on the other! How therefore, does this give us any reason to view our understanding of the world as being in line with how it actually *is*?

Perhaps a better way to characterise what is going on is to say that our brains and our science work in tandem to give us a picture of the world, but that there is no way of stepping past this picture and seeing the universe's true nature. Science, rather than giving us an understanding of the world, only gives us an understanding of our experiences. It is allowing us to gain a deeper insight into the picture of the world produced by our brains, and gives us some control and predictive power over what experiences our brains may give us in the future. But it is not telling us anything about the true nature of the universe – all we have is models.

Science gives us one model of the world around us – an explicit, abstract model that we humans have consciously constructed. This contrasts with the immediate picture, or model, of the world that our brains continually create for us, that needs no artificial intervention. Yet ultimately, it's all models of one sort or another.

*

We have worked hard to get to this recognition, tackling some notoriously difficult subjects along the way. However, I would say that we are now equipped with the tools we need to be able to finally answer the question of whether or not God exists. This is our next job.

PART II – HEIST

The map *is* the territory

Chapter 10

10. The Map *is* the Territory

Following all the work done in Part I, we are now in a position to make the case that 'All the world is models' and see where this takes us in answering some of the big questions such as 'What is consciousness?', 'Could solipsism be true?' and 'Does God exist?'.

Let's start then, with the claim that Descartes overreached himself by saying he could be certain that he existed. We said that the question of what I can know to be real involves three separate concepts: the self (the 'I'), one's experiences (the things that may or may not be real) and independent reality (the set of things that are indeed real). We then noted that all I really know for sure is that I am having experiences – this idea of independent reality is a third thing, a metaphysical concept, and we have no justification for believing it even exists. This implies that the concept of independent reality is a *theory* that we come up with to help make sense of our experiences. We don't normally realise that it's only a theory, because our brains give us this model subconsciously. But downstream theories, such as the laws of science, or Kant's metaphysics are founded on this base level theory that there is an independent reality. An alternative base level theory is available, namely that there is no independent reality and our experiences are all that there is – solipsism.

The Solipsist Case

The first decision to be taken then, in order to make sense of our experiences, is whether to adopt a solipsist model. If one has to imagine what it would be like living with such a model, then this is none too easy a thing to do, for all of the understanding we are given growing up, not to mention the models given to us subconsciously by our brains, take an independent reality for granted. We'd have to somehow convince ourselves that a golf ball really does disappear when moved into the blind spot and that when we turn around, the world we were looking at literally ceases to exist. To get around this problem, a solipsist may claim that we experience things *as though* there is an independent reality. Our brains model the world as still existing even when our eyes are closed, and our scientific theories take it as a given that there is an independent 'real world'. However this then puts the solipsist in the almost self-contradictory position of saying 'I find the best way of understanding my experiences is to use a model which says there is no independent reality even though the universe behaves in line with a model that says there is one'. The solipsistic component of such a model is empty. You may as well cut to the chase and use a model that says there is an independent reality.

The case for adopting a solipsist model therefore seems weak. But what if it's true? Let's suppose for completeness then, that solipsism is true and so you are the only thing that exists. Can you obtain an answer to the question of whether God exists?

Well we can immediately answer that God, as an all-powerful and good being separate from you, and independent of you[25], does not exist, because nothing exists independently of you. On the other hand, it might be said that God could exist in some other sense. Through life, you interact with objects of your experience that you call 'tables' and 'chairs' for example. And perhaps you pray to a God of sorts. This God cannot have created

[25] Not to be confused with Kant's transcendental objects, which are separate from the subject, but still dependent on the subject for their existence

you, because that would mean God is an independent being. However, God could perhaps be thought of as something that can affect your experiences. Just as you can affect the nature of your experience by choosing to walk around the house in a different direction, to use Kant's example, you may also affect your experiences by praying. If you call the focal point of your prayers 'God', then you have provided a label for a part of your model of the nature of your experience. If solipsism were true, you could model your experiences in terms of tables and chairs and, perhaps, God, even if they do not exist in an independent reality. The idea of God may be more abstract than the ideas of tables and chairs, but it is still part of the way you could model your experiences.

What do we mean by existence? If the solipsist position is true, then no objects really exist, so the term becomes redundant – it cannot usefully be applied to anything. A more useful and practical definition of existence might be to say that something exists if it is treated as existing. Everything that features in experience is as real as everything else, so if there is an experiences of ghosts, then they are just as real as experiences of tables and chairs. What else is there to assess existence against, when there is no independent reality – no 'real world'? On this definition of existence, it is reasonable to say that anything that appears to exist, does indeed exist.

What if the solipsist understands the concept of God, but doesn't believe in him? Are we saying that because God features in their thinking, then he exists? We are not. Here we would say that if they don't consider that this concept has any bearing on how events actually pan out, then God doesn't exist as more than just a concept. Under solipsism, someone who doesn't believe in God, is someone saying that they don't consider it appropriate to feature this concept as part of their model of the behaviour of their experiences. Again, the reality is identical to your perception of it.

Now let's move on and consider the alternative case where there *is* an independent reality.

In the Real World

If Immanuel Kant's arguments are convincing, then it must be accepted that an understanding of how independent reality is structured is impossible. And even for philosophers who refuse to accept Kant's arguments and insist on a scientific realist view, we saw that an understanding of how independent reality is structured is also impossible in practice, because any theory could always turn out to be wrong in the future (in Karl Popper's phrase, it could be 'falsified'). To keep this point at the forefront of our thinking in the discussion ahead, I suggest that we might alternatively call independent reality '*the Superunknowable*'.

With that in mind, let's return to the central question of whether God exists. Can we identify whether there is really a God that lies behind our impression of him existing (or our impression that he does not exist as the case may be)? But before we pose such a question of God, let's start by asking it of something simpler like an aeroplane. Suppose you look out of the window and there, up in the sky, you see an aeroplane. Does this aeroplane actually exist? Or is it an illusion or a figment of your imagination or are you dreaming? If it exists, we are saying that behind your perception that there is an aeroplane in the sky, lies the actual aeroplane as it is in itself[26]. If you were not in attendance, looking at it, this does not cause the aeroplane to disappear. It has a concrete reality of its own.

To make progress, let's consider two different scenarios. In the first scenario, the aeroplane does indeed exist – it is an actual aeroplane that I am seeing. In the second scenario, the aeroplane does not exist – though I believe I am seeing an aeroplane, it is actually something else.

I can understand the concept of an aeroplane. I look at the sky and receive sensory impressions that my brain uses to construct a particular phenomenon. I recognise this phenomenon as an aeroplane. In the first scenario, my perception matches the underlying object which is an

---

[26] The thing as it is in itself, or more simply 'the thing in itself' is common philosophical parlance for the thing as it exists in independent reality – as it is independently of any subjective features.

aeroplane, and so I am correct in identifying the phenomenon as an aeroplane. In the second scenario, I was mistaken. The sensory impressions actually stemmed from something that should have been interpreted as, say, a bird or a mirage, rather than an aeroplane.

What is the difference between those two scenarios? In both, we have an independent reality, which may have some kind of structure, but is ultimately unknowable. This is key. Scientific enquiry can model how the world around us behaves, but it cannot reveal the structure of reality itself. Also in both, the object provokes a phenomenon which is interpreted by the observer as an aeroplane. The two situations are therefore, in terms of the objective facts, *exactly the same!* The only difference between the two scenarios is that in Scenario 1, we labelled the unknowable thing in itself an aeroplane and in Scenario 2, we labelled it a bird. But given that the unknowable thing in itself is, not to put too fine a point on it, unknowable, we have no grounds for distinguishing between the two scenarios. The idea that there is a difference between scenarios one and two therefore results from a misunderstanding of what can be known about independent reality. In both scenarios, there was an unknowable independent reality and we looked up into the sky and saw what we interpreted as an aeroplane.

At this point, it might be tempting to object that there is another difference between the two scenarios. In Scenario 1, even if we don't understand exactly how it is structured, the underlying object is an aeroplane, whereas in Scenario 2, it is a bird. We give them different labels because they *are* different things – they have different structures. And these different structures would normally give rise to different phenomena in our minds – it is only because the object was so far away that we struggled to tell whether it was a bird or an aeroplane. If the phenomenon was provoked by a bird, then although it looked the same as an aeroplane in that moment, it is fundamentally different. This matters because it might start to flap its wings for example, whereas an aeroplane will not.

However, this objection doesn't go anywhere. We are not disputing the idea that the nature of the phenomenon is driven by the nature of the underlying object. Only the solipsist rejects the idea that our experiences have an external source. We are just saying that because the nature of the thing in itself is hidden from us, we cannot look to the nature of the thing in itself to help us understand our environment. In Scenario 2, the observer experiences a phenomenon that is provoked by an underlying object, that they label an aeroplane. A few seconds later, the 'aeroplane' flaps its wings and the observer realises their error and now recognises it as a bird. Whether the object is a bird or a plane has been determined by the way it appears, and by this physical evidence only. The nature of the underlying object has had no impact on the situation.

It is tempting to think that if we had a scientific theory that would help us understand the underlying objects, this would allow us to better understand the phenomena that we actually experience. If only we could directly inspect the underlying object, then would know that our phenomenon was a bird without having to wait for it to flap its wings! Unfortunately, we are limited by our humanity and only have access to our experiences. Science can only inspect and model phenomena, with no reference to any underlying objects. As mentioned in chapter 8, it is important not to confuse these underlying objects, with postulated entities such as atoms and fundamental particles which are part of our models and so belong to the world of phenomena.

It is worth spending a few moments considering what we mean when we use the term 'aeroplane'. Are we referring to the phenomenon – the aeroplane as it appears to me, or the aeroplane as it is in itself? There is a long history of discussion in philosophy around how words get their meaning, but ultimately, as pointed out by Wittgenstein in his Philosophical Investigations, words mean what people use them to mean[xxxvi].

For example, what do I mean when I use the term 'blue'? Now you might think you can picture the quality of blueness in your mind, but given that this image is private to you, it is difficult to convey what you mean by the quality of blueness to others. When I explain to a toddler what I mean by the colour blue, I do it by picking out examples. I am talking about the quality that things like the sky and the sea have in common. So if I say the grass is blue, am I right or wrong? Wittgenstein points out that the reason I am wrong is that the term is not used in that way. If there was no-one else on the planet, I could quite easily define 'blue' to mean the quality that the sky, the sea and grass have in common and I would be correct to say that grass is blue! It might seem strange to speakers of English to think that there could hypothetically be any scenario where one could accept that the grass is blue, but in other languages this is the case. In Gaelic, grass is often referred to as gorm[27], even though gorm more commonly translates as blue. And even in English, are the sea and the sky really the same colour?

Meaning is derived through usage. Now at this point, someone might object that 'blue' refers to the particular frequencies of light reflected off the item in question. And so, I would still be wrong to say that grass is blue, even if there was no-one else on the planet, because grass reflects different frequencies of light to those reflected by the sky and the sea. But again, this is just about usage. The term 'blue' has expanded its meaning to incorporate particular frequencies of light, through the way people use the term.

Let's get back to aeroplanes. We said 'aeroplane' could perhaps refer to both the phenomenon of the aeroplane and the object as it is in itself lying behind this phenomenon. But the word 'aeroplane' as used publicly refers to an object that is big, shiny, hard, flies in the sky and doesn't flap its wings. This all reflects how we perceive it and so is a description of a phenomenon. It makes no sense to talk about an aeroplane as an underlying object – the underlying aeroplane is stripped of all the properties that make it an aeroplane in the first place and becomes a shadowy thing lying out of sight.

One might be tempted at this point argue that the aeroplane as it is in itself, is the atoms and molecules that make it up, that exist independently of my perception of it. I might perceive that collection of atoms and molecules differently from the way a dog does, but it is the configuration

[27] Pronounced 'gorrum'

of these atoms and molecules that determines the form of the object as it is in itself. However this argument is misleading. Atoms and molecules are components of scientific models and therefore form part of the world of phenomena, in its broad sense of referring to the objects that we perceive and our understanding of them. They are part of our *model* of reality; we cannot know if reality really is structured that way. We cannot know what the aeroplane as it is in itself is 'really like'.

We don't know anything about the structure of the underlying object in Scenarios 1 and 2, and it isn't accurate to label it either 'bird' or 'aeroplane' because these terms only have meaning at the everyday level. Fundamentally the structure of underlying reality is not relevant, as the factors that give our lives meaning do not operate at that level. All we have is the phenomena and our (e.g. scientific) models. Independent reality (assuming it exists), may be three dimensional, four dimensional or ten dimensional. It doesn't matter. We experience it as three dimensional and that is the reality that we are faced with. The outside world might be populated with trillions of invisible pink ghost unicorns; it doesn't matter. This is not what we perceive. This is not what we interact with. What is crucial to understand is that when trying to figure out what independent reality is 'really like', is that the world that we perceive and our scientific theories are the end of the line. Independent reality is not a reality we can ever know. It is always shrouded behind the veil of phenomena and our models. So it doesn't matter what structure the object underlying the aeroplane phenomenon has – we are still experiencing an aeroplane. We can therefore now discard this double meaning of the word 'aeroplane' as referring to both the phenomenon and the underlying 'real' object that we introduced above.

Where does this leave us? In Scenario 1, we have a perceived aeroplane, behind which lies an unknowable object and in Scenario 2, we have a perceived aeroplane, also behind which lies an unknowable object. From our perspective, the situation is the same – the fact that the underlying object is unknowable means that it is impossible for us to distinguish between the two scenarios.

There is one final point to make before bringing the discussion back to the existence of God. Because we don't know anything about the underlying objects, one of the things we don't know is what phenomenon any particular underlying object is provoking. It is not even clear if there is a one-to-one correspondence between phenomenal objects and underlying objects. Where does one object end and another begin? This may seem straightforward at the macroscopic level, when thinking about books lying on tables, but not always. For example where is the edge of a cloud?

Whenever you climb a big hill and try to get up into the clouds, the cloud always seems to recede away from you and remain a few tens of meters out of reach. Even though, to someone standing on the ground, you are clearly inside the cloud. Now one could argue that on top of a cloud covered hill, I am surrounded by condensed, seeded droplets of water and so am indeed inside the cloud, even if it doesn't appear that way to me. But is that really what we mean by cloud in everyday usage? We use the word cloud to describe the situation where those droplets are densely packed enough to appear opaque – again these words are really only meaningful at the level of appearances. If we look up at the sky, we can see the edges of the clouds, even though in reality there is no hard boundary between the part of the sky that contains the seeded condensed water droplets and the part of the sky that does not.

What about at the sub-atomic level? How big is an electron? Where is the edge of a black hole? And what do we even mean by an object in the context of independent reality? How do forces and energy fit in? The idea that independent reality has a structure of discrete objects A, B and C etc which neatly correspond to the objects we perceive as phenomena is not something that can be taken for granted. It is a macroscopic idea that makes sense to us as humans, but, as we saw when trying to apply the macroscopic planetary model to the world of the atom, the world outside our everyday experience can be very strange. We therefore cannot assume that there is an individual object, or even a collection of objects, within underlying reality that corresponds to the aeroplane we perceive as a phenomenon. The idea that underlying reality is comprised of a number of distinct underlying objects is a *model* of underlying reality. Claiming that as a fact of underlying reality is dogmatic – we have no grounds for doing so.

So how it this relevant to the existence of God? Initially we naively thought that the question was whether or not there was a real, underlying God that is part of the real independent reality that causes our impression, (the phenomenon) of God existing (or despite our impression of God not existing, if we are an unbeliever). However, we have now seen that the answer is not 'yes' or 'no', because the question makes no sense. We have just seen that we cannot divide underlying reality into 'God' and 'Not-God' objects, as this would be to say something about its structure, which we have already seen is unknowable. We cannot give labels such as 'God' to underlying objects, because that would be to assign properties to these objects, whereas we have seen that the concept of properties only makes sense in the world of phenomena. So the actual situation is as follows: As an individual, you may believe in God, in the sense that you experience the universe as though he exists. Or you may not. Behind the scenes, we have the Superunknowable – an independent reality with a structure that is unknowable, but that leads to the reality that we experience. Just as with the aeroplane, we cannot look to the structure of independent reality to understand the reality that we experience because we cannot ever know or understand independent reality.

We find that the situation is the same as that discussed above. Independent reality is an unknowable mystery – all we have to live by is our overall picture of reality. Attempting to discuss the existence of specific underlying objects is a dead end. The only useful definition of existence is the existence of certain phenomena or objects-for-us. This therefore comes down to a practical consideration of whether God plays any role in your life. It makes no sense to talk about God at the level of underlying objects (things-in-themselves). Like aeroplanes and birds, the features that make God God are only applicable at the level of phenomena or objects of experience.

What, though, if someone held a strongly scientific realist view and argued that although independent reality is unknowable, it *could* still have a god, even if we could never know for sure one way or the other? We have seen that this possibility is ultimately irrelevant, as it has no bearing on the world as we can know or experience it. It has no impact on our lives. We saw when examining the reasonableness of convergent realism, that we could come up with a Theory of Everything, an understanding of how the world works, which always turns out to be in line with our experiences – all its predictions turn out to be correct to within the accuracy that we can measure – that is different to how the world actually is. And we could never be aware of this. This Theory of Everything would be the world we live by – whether the structure of this theory is a match to the structure of the Superunknowable – underlying independent reality – is academic. So what are the implications if the Superunknowable has an intelligible structure and this structure contains God? In this case, one might expect that best way to understand our experiences would be to have God in our model – our understanding – of how the world works. However, if our model works perfectly fine, for us, with no God in it, then whether there is a God as part of the Superunknowable is irrelevant. Remember we have shown that there is no benefit to having a double-meaning for object words. If God doesn't exist as part of your model, that is the end of the story – whether or not God can or does exist as part of the Superunknowable is moot. In that sense Independent Reality with a structure is just the Trendelenburg Alternative from chapter 8 – we can't reach it, it can't impact us and any similarities in structure would be a sheer coincidence.

So perhaps the appropriate question is not 'Does God exist?' which has no meaning in practice. The better question may be instead 'Do you have a God?' Your experience, which has tables and chairs and aeroplanes – does it also have God? The way we make sense of our experience *is* our reality – by default. Independent reality is unknowable (if it even exists), so the only de facto reality is our set of experiences and the framework or model that we use to make sense of them. Our understanding of our experiences – of Life, the Universe and Everything – cannot rest on an understanding of how independent reality is structured, because at best, such knowledge is forever beyond us and at worst, it doesn't even make sense to consider it as something that can be understood, even in principle.

When the scientific realist asks 'Does God exist', he or she is really wanting an answer to the question 'Does the correct model of independent reality include God?'. This presupposes both that there is such a thing as an independent reality and that it has an intelligible form. And we have seen that even if you grant these two presuppositions, the question is impossible to answer. But we can also now recognise that it is a technical question that is irrelevant to the main issue. What we really want to know is 'Does the God that we might know and interact with every day really exist?' To answer this main question, we need to look at our model of reality. Let's say we have Rhian who is an atheist. She accepts that there is an independent reality, but it makes sense to her that there is no God. Then we have Iain. He finds that God responds to his prayers and God plays a big part in his life. Finally, we have Liam. Let's say Liam is a solipsist. In his view, there is nothing apart from him and his experiences and let's suppose that that works for him. Who has the correct model of reality? Again, we can never know and it may not even make sense to ask. 'Aha!' you say. 'What about on death? Then we will finally have the big reveal!

Or will we? Let's say Rhian the atheist dies. Drum roll... Rhian sees God and goes to heaven! God exists! Praise Be! Fanfare! At least, that is Rhian's experience. But let's bear in mind the people who have direct religious experiences and 'see God' whilst still alive. Can she know that this is really what is happening? Rhian might think that actually, this after-death experience is best explained as some kind of dream and that she is not really dead. Or if she is dead, can she be sure that her continuing awareness is a result of God's intervention? Might Rhian plump for a more scientific explanation instead? Perhaps, with the body no longer functioning in normal space, the architecture of consciousness has somehow been transferred to a structure in other dimensions? Does God need to be involved? 'After all', says Rhian, 'Where was God when I was alive?' Ultimately, we cannot know independent reality and so we need to explain our experiences as best we can by whatever models work for us (even after death!). If Rhian lives and dies with the model that God doesn't exist, then whether there technically is a God in the Superunknowable (assuming that it even makes sense to ask that question) is academic and irrelevant to real life.

It is human nature to worry that our model might be wrong and that if it doesn't feature God, we may come to regret it in the future. This is perhaps what motivated Pascal when he proposed the wager discussed earlier. Recall that Pascal recommended believing in God because if you don't and it turns out that he does exist, then you will be cast into the fiery pits of Hell for all eternity. But there may be another possibility that Pascal overlooked. It could be that there is no God, just the invisible pink ghost unicorns from chapter 7. And it may turn out that these ghost unicorns can only interact with the dead and what they despise most of all is those who believe in God. Pascal is caught between a rock and a hard place. Irrespective of whether he believes in God or the unicorns, if he gets it wrong, he is in trouble.

But it is easy to cook up invisible bogeymen that are out to get you. There are an infinite number of different possible Gods, powers and forces that could constitute the way that the Superunknowable is actually configured, so it seems crazy to paralyse yourself with worry over which one might be right, when such knowledge is beyond us. It's a bit like being afraid of the dark. Who knows what will happen in the future that is not predicted by our model of reality? We do the best we can, and the reality that is meaningful to us is the model by which we live, irrespective of how thing are constructed beyond the veil.

So if we are looking for a simple answer to the question of whether God exists, the best answer is probably 'mu'. Mu is an ancient Japanese word, that means 'neither yes, nor no'. It means that the question makes no sense or that it pre-supposes certain facts that are not true and so any answer that takes the question at face value is wrong. An oft-quoted example is the question 'have you stopped beating your wife?' This would appear to be the appropriate response for us, because to ask 'Does God Exist?' pre-supposes the common-sense picture – a scientific realist picture of reality that we have shown to be unsupportable[xxxvii].

Does God exist?

Mu

We have seen that in both the solipsist universe, where there is just our experience, and the universe where there is an independent reality that lies behind our experience, to speak of God existing in a meaningful way is to say that he features as part of the map or model you use to make sense of your experiences. The fact that irrespective of which of these two positions holds, you end up in the same place is perhaps not surprising, given that it is our experiences that are primary. It is the same experiences that we are modelling in both cases – whether there is, or is not, an unknowable independent reality, is a question without significance, like that of the existence of the invisible pink ghost unicorns.

Furthermore, it could be argued that as well as the solipsist question having no practical significance, it is also badly formed. I previously introduced the concept of solipsism with the question 'Would there be anything left if you were removed from the totally of all that exists?' To answer this question, we need to consider the perspective from which it is asked. If it is a question about independent reality, asked from the perspective of our disembodied camera, then to ask if there is more to reality than just you, is to credit it with a certain structure. It takes it as given that reality can be considered as a set of items that includes you and possibly other things – in this case the sources of your experiences. But we now know that to say that independent reality has a particular structure, is to say something that cannot be known. To borrow from Wittgenstein (who was in turn borrowing from Weinenger), 'what we cannot speak about, we must pass over in silence'. Certainly, we each exist from our own perspective, but it can't be said with any certainty that we exist in reality as a thing-in-itself. We can't objectively be separated from the rest of reality – the most that could be said is that we are a kind of expression of reality. Put another way, you and everything that you see are a perspective on reality.

On the other hand, from the perspective of the individual, when asking if there would be anything left if you – meaning your individual consciousness – were removed, we need to consider whether we are talking about the greater or lesser 'you'. If we are talking about the greater you – not just your body, but your full experiences and point of view, then there would obviously be nothing left – everything that exists relies on you for its form. From the point of view of what you see, if everything you see is removed, including the you that does the seeing, there is nothing left for you to see, not least because there is no you to do any seeing. On the other hand, if we were talking about the you in your model – the you that is distinct from the objects of your experience, then the model says that those objects still remain. This is the everyday sense of this question – asked from within the framework of your model. But it is important to stress that this is only a hypothetical question – the objects as they are formed in the model cannot continue to exist without the entity that sustains that form.

So I would argue that in order for the solipsist question to have any value, then it needs to be asked from the perspectiveless perspective – as a question about independent reality. But this is exactly the perspective from which the question cannot be asked, because it presupposes that independent reality has a certain form and this cannot be known.

*

It is helpful to think of our scientific theories and the picture of the world that we have in our minds as a map of reality. Like any map, it does not contain the full detail of the territory that it is attempting to map out. Like our brains do, the map will just highlight the key areas that matter most. And so when using a map for navigational purposes, it is important to bear in mind the famous maxim 'The map is not the territory'. This reminds us that the map will not contain the full detail of how the land before us is laid out and that these differences can be important.

However, when it comes to our map of reality, the map is *all we have*. The territory – the world of independent reality, underlying our perceptions and models of it, is unknown and inaccessible to us. It is like hill-running in the clouds or sailing a boat at night, relying solely on the navigational instruments such as GPS, the radar and depth gauge, when the rocks, cliffs and lie of the land are invisible to you.

Scientific realism as a world view, has dominated serious thought for over a century. However, recent advances in neuroscience support a view that the world as generated by the brain is best thought of as a kind of controlled hallucination. I am hopeful that such developments may help to restore the credibility of idealist philosophies and expose the dogma inherent in the realist position. Once it is understood that its goal of understanding the true nature of independent reality is beyond reach, then scientific realism becomes a positive hindrance to the goal of understanding whether or not God exists. Firstly it is dogmatic because it takes for granted that there is an independent reality. Secondly, it assumes that this independent reality can in principle be understood, which we saw was far from clear. And thirdly and finally we saw that even if we accept the idea that there is an independent reality that has a comprehensible structure, the structure itself is academic – it is only the models that have a bearing on the reality that we experience.

This led us to think again about what we mean by saying that something exists. We are considering one of these phenomena; an object that forms part of our map, that we interact with, such as an aeroplane or God. Does it really exist? Our old definition said that something exists if it corresponds to an underlying object in independent reality. But we have now seen that this is a dead end. We cannot know anything about independent reality. In fact the objects of independent reality pass pretty much every test of non-existence you can think of. Can we perceive them directly? No. Can we perceive them indirectly i.e. can we infer that they exist based on their effect on other things? No. We cannot even know if independent reality is made up of distinct objects that neatly correspond to our everyday phenomenal objects of experience. The existence of a set of independent real objects, or 'things as they are in themselves', is no more than an idea, a collection of shadowy things lying out of sight, which, as a concept, might help some people to explain their experiences. For something to exist, for something to be real, we need a bit more than it merely existing as a concept. If we want to understand whether God exists in the same way that this book in front of me exists, we can see that an appeal to the nature of independent reality is not going to help.

To sum up, the structure of reality, inasmuch as it is meaningful to us, is therefore in terms of the model we use to make sense of it. We have seen that this is as true in the solipsist case, as it is in the case where there is such a thing as an independent reality – supporting Wittgenstein's assertion that a nothing will do as well as a something about which nothing can be said. How you make sense of your experiences may be different to how I make sense of mine, but they don't have to agree. You can select a metaphysics, a model, that works for you. This may or may not include a God – in that respect, anything goes, as long as it works for you in making sense your experiences.

PART III – GETAWAY

Anything Goes

Chapter 11

11. Man is the Measure of All Things

Physics and philosophy are sometimes compared to mountain climbing, in that it takes a lot of hard work to get to your goal, but, once you do, the satisfaction of seeing the world anew in a different light can be likened to the new physical perspective offered by the views from the mountain top.

However, just getting to the summit is not the end of the journey, whether exploring the Himalayas or philosophical puzzles. Just as climbers must make their way back down the mountain, explorers in the territory of the mind must find a way back from the new insight – and in both cases this can be no less challenging than the climb. Indeed, it has been claimed that more mountaineers have died during the descent of Mount Everest than the ascent. From a philosophical perspective, coming back down the mountain means considering what the implications of our new understanding are for the way we see the rest of the world around us.

At this point, despite the slabs of logic from Part II appearing to fall into place in a watertight checkmate, it is possible that some people may still be reluctant to let go of what they feel to be common sense scientific realist beliefs. Yes, they may find the lack of an accessible world of underlying concrete objects common to all of us disorientating, but perhaps the biggest issue that the analysis in Part II raises is the problem of error. If I believe that what I saw was an aeroplane and you believe it was a bird, then surely we can't both be right? But how can this be resolved if there is no knowable independent reality for us to refer to as arbiter of truth? After all, isn't a consequence of the Anything Goes result in Part II that we now have a licence to claim that anything we want to believe to be true, is actually true?[28] We can call it the Anything Goes approach, with capital letters to make it clear that we are referring specifically to the thinking explored in the Part II, which relates to a metaphysical framework for our experiences, rather than a general claim that there are no limitations on which statements about the world are true.

A related question is whether the Anything Goes approach provides room for doubt. If 'the map is the territory', does this not suggest that since we can read the map, everything is clear to us. Where is the room for unknowns in this picture? If the world cannot be configured meaningfully outside the way I perceive it to be, does it make sense to say that there is anything meaningful outside of what I already believe? If I don't know who stole the money, then my map is not able to model who stole the money – does that therefore mean there was no thief? Some people might argue that the Anything Goes approach destroys the gap between what *is* the case and what *can be known* to be the case.

Unfortunately, saying 'I don't like the consequences and so the arguments must be flawed' is unsatisfactory if the actual flaws in the arguments cannot be pointed out. Wittgenstein once stated that his aim in philosophy was to show the fly the way out of the fly bottle – that is to say, to help people disentangle themselves from the confusions that they find themselves in when they try to apply various concepts inappropriately. In this third part of the book, I want to explore some of the confusions that result from the scientific realist way of thinking and show that the Anything Goes approach can provide a much more satisfactory way of seeing things.

---

[28] There are a number of 'anti-realist' schools of thought which proceed along these lines. I will explore in the next few chapters whether it is reasonable to argue that the lack of an independent reality to which truths correspond means that any logically consistent statement can be claimed to be true.

Meaning and Reference

Let's start with the problem of error. I have proposed that 'all the world is models', so on this logic if I believe I am perceiving a bird when you say it is a plane then we can both be right in our views and can claim with justification that whatever we believe to be true is indeed true! At which point, it seems that something has gone very wrong somewhere. To address this, the first question we might ask is how do we know we are talking about the *same* object, if there is no single common underlying object that we are discussing? Now we saw when discussing a conversation about an object that is blue, that even if our private experiences of how this object appears are different, we can still have a meaningful conversation about it. This may provide us with a promising way to establish some objectivity or agreed common ground for our experiences.

Suppose we both see an object and we both label it an aeroplane. My experience of the aeroplane might be different to yours, for example because I am colourblind or am looking at it from a different angle. If there is no underlying, independently real aeroplane, then what do my aeroplane and your aeroplane have in common to allow us to know that we are talking about the same thing? The thing that they have in common is the label that we apply to the object. Both of us call it an aeroplane.

In order to understand how this helps us move forward, we need to consider what we mean by the term 'aeroplane'. Perhaps the first place to go to find out the meaning of words is the dictionary. After all, this is what dictionaries are for. However, there are a few problems with this. Firstly, can we be sure that the dictionary is up to date? The meaning of words appears to change over time – we can look at words like 'nail' or 'bark' with double meanings, or words like 'perversion' which used to simply mean a difference from the norm, but now has a more pejorative meaning. Furthermore, are all words in the dictionary? What about new words like 'selfie' or slang, like 'plaction'? If a word is not in the dictionary, does that mean it is meaningless? Of course, we know that the role of the dictionary is less about instructing society on what words mean and more about recording the meaning of words, which society already has stored within its body of collective knowledge.

The philosophy of language and meaning goes back at least as far as Plato but became a particularly hot topic at the start of the 20th Century. Philosophers recognised that our everyday language was woolly – full of blurred edges and subtleties where one word may have several meanings or different meanings in different contexts. The challenge was on to try to create a more idealised, or precise, language which had the ambiguity of everyday speech stripped away. This lead to the popularisation of a 'referentialist' view of word meaning, advanced by philosophers such as Gottlob Frege and Bertrand Russell[xxxviii]. Referentialism takes as a starting point a child's language learning, which is viewed essentially as a correlation of words and objects. In its basic form, Referentialism then formalises this by asserting that the meaning of a word *is* the object to which it refers. So for example, the meaning of the word 'Sun' is the star around which our planet revolves. 'Hund' (in German), 'cù' (in Gaelic) and 'chien' (in French) all refer to what we call a 'dog' in English, but this is slightly more problematic because there is no single object in the world to which this word refers. But what about words like 'unicorn', of which there are no examples? And things get even more difficult with words like 'justice', 'love', 'pain' or the number five. Where in the world are the objects to which these words refer?

However, it might perhaps only be important to establish that words stand for *something*, some abstract object, even if not specific objects in the world. This will allow us to be clear that 'bring me the stone' means the same as 'thoir dhomh a' chlach' – both 'bring' and 'thoir' refer to the action of bringing, 'me' and 'dhomh' both refer to the speaker and both 'the stone' and 'a' chlach' refer to a particular stone. Otherwise, philosophers might worry, how can we be sure that what I mean when I say 'bring me the stone' is the same as what you understand it to mean when you hear me say it? This assurance could be provided if the logical form of language reflected the logical form of the underlying reality it is supposed to represent. 'But what is the logical form of *that*?' (the underlying reality), challenged Italian economist Piero Sraffa, when Wittgenstein was defending this view[29]. We have already seen that the only reality that can have any known structure is just a model – a description. On this basis, language would be a description of a description. Reality as it is in itself is unknowable and so attempting to ground language on a structure which is unknowable is a dead end.

Where do we go from here? This might be a worry for philosophers, but it needn't worry anyone else. Ludwig Wittgenstein came to the rescue by emphasizing that the meaning of words in a language emerges through their *usage*. If I go to a market stall and say I want five apples, we might see the market trader placing apples, one at a time, into a bag, counting as they do – 'one', 'two', 'three', 'four', 'five' and stopping at that point. Both of us are happy that we know the meaning of the word 'five', not because it refers to some abstract object, but because we know from experience how to use it.

The key point here, it is argued, is that although our experiences of the aeroplane may be different, our descriptions of them will be the same. If we are talking about the same flower, our descriptions have to be the same by definition; otherwise it is not the same flower. How do we know if we are talking about the same thing?

"Look at that flower over there"
"Which one?"
"The big blue one"
"Ah yes, I see it"

We both know how to use the terms, 'big', 'blue' and 'flower' because we've seen them used many times before. This coherent conversation provides the common ground for the object in question. Or more simply, this coherent conversation makes it clear that we are talking about the same thing. This is the case, even under the common-sense picture! If we want to be sure we are talking about the same thing, we just describe it. We don't try to refer to some underlying object, as it exists independently of

[29] Wittgenstein's mature views in his 'Philosophical Investigations' differ sharply from this position and are outlined in the paragraphs ahead.

our perceptions. The common description provides the guarantee that we are talking about the same object.

The reason this works is that the meaning of words such as 'blue' and 'big' are dictated by how they are used, not by the experiences that they correspond to. It is an operational definition. A colourblind person may not know how you experience blueness, so how could the meaning of 'blue' be explained to you in terms of your experience? Instead, as noted earlier, we learn the meaning of 'blue' through its use. It is what the sea and the sky have in common.

In contrast, imagine two people in their own separate worlds, conversing over some kind of inter-dimensional coms link.

"Look at that flower over there"
"Which one?"
"The big blue one"
"What are you talking about? I only see little red ones"

We might close by noting that even under the realist view, the referentialist theory of meaning doesn't really work. If I talk of a large blue flower, I talk of phenomenal properties, even under the realist perspective. The guarantee that we are talking about the same thing is not provided by the underlying object, even in the realist world, as this does not have any features that can be described. Rather, our agreement that we are talking about the same object is based on us using the same label; on agreeing about its description.

What do we Mean when we say that an Object Exists?

Let's apply this to resolve the Problem of Error by considering a scenario similar to that outlined in Part II. We both see an object in the sky; I think it's an aeroplane and you think it's a bird. Surely, here we are talking about the same object but *disagreeing* about its label? Under the Anything Goes approach, we are both right, so how do we resolve this?

When we look at this object, our brains are giving us a model of how the world really is. I am modelling it as an aeroplane and if you tell me you think it is a bird, then since you are part of my world, I think you are wrong, and so out come the binoculars. I see the 'aeroplane' flap its wings and so the data is no longer consistent with my model of the object being an aeroplane and the inconsistency is resolved. But under this Anything Goes school of metaphysics, I was right a second ago, saying it was an aeroplane, even though I am also right now in saying it is a bird. How can that be? There are two options. Either a) the aeroplane turned into a bird at the point I pulled out the binoculars or b) it always was a bird and I was wrong previously.

As always, I am looking for a model of my experiences that gives me the best understanding of them. Option (a) seems to involve an unlikely coincidence, and in addition I have no explanation as to how an aeroplane can suddenly turn into a bird. It raises the possibility that any object could suddenly change form without warning and so all predictive power about the future is lost, which in turn means I have no certainty or feeling of control over my surroundings. Option (b) on the other hand, is consistent with all the other things I think I know about reality, and so is preferable. By pursuing Option (b), I am resetting my model and applying my updated model retrospectively to now say that I was wrong before.

This is not too different to the way we go about understanding the world under the scientific realist picture. It is just that instead of believing that we correct ourselves when we get a better understanding of the way the world 'really is', we correct ourselves when we get a better model. A better model doesn't need to be anything revolutionary. Any model has both form and content and both are required for an output – for understanding. If I get new data – I see the object flap its wings – this is new content and the output of my model is that it is a bird, rather than a plane. Note the parallels with Kant, who argued that the form of our reality is based on our humanity, with the content coming from an independent reality.

But, what about if we had no binoculars and one believes it is a bird and the other believes it is a plane? By virtue of the fact that in principle, if we were able to observe the object through binoculars, we would obtain sufficient appropriate evidence to resolve it into either a bird or a plane, we go for the idea that one of us is in error, we just don't yet know which one of us that is. But strictly speaking, under the Anything Goes school of metaphysics, neither of us is mistaken at the time because there is no common criterion by which to judge error, even in principle. There is no independent object that it 'really' is. All there is is experience and models. Note that there is no inconsistency in saying that I was right before to claim it was an aeroplane and I am also right now to claim that I was wrong before. This is because the before and after assessments are made against different models. This point will be discussed further in the next chapter.

Can we use a parallel argument in the situation where we have two people, one of whom explains their experiences in terms of God and one who does not? In this situation, however powerful your binoculars, they will not help. The disagreement is not to do with the content of the model, it is to do with the form. It makes no sense to argue 'I don't know whether God exists because I don't yet have enough data'. So in these situations, how do we determine whether such statements about the world are true or false? This will be discussed in the next chapter.

Chapter 12

12. Another Copernican Revolution

Consider some questions like "is it true that $5 + 7 = 12$?". Or "is it true that Paris is the capital of France?". There seems to be no difficulty in deciding on the truth or otherwise of these questions. What about "Is it true that the world is round?" On the face of it, most people in the 21st century would say yes. But the surface of the earth is not smooth – what about all the mountain ranges? Ah, but if you include the atmosphere as well, then the surface is smooth. So it depends what you mean by the 'earth'. But what about the fact that the diameter of the earth is greater at the equator than at the poles? Then the earth is not spherical; it is more like a three dimensional oval. Is an oval round?

So we can see that the truth or otherwise of a statement depends very much on the meaning of the terms within it. And if different words mean different things to different people, what does that mean with regard to statements being universally true? Is Glasgow a big city?

An important distinction between different types of truth goes back to Gottfried Leibniz (1646-1716). The German philosopher divided our knowledge between truths of reason and truths of fact. Truths of fact are verified by reference to experience. For example, the truth or otherwise of the statement 'the sky is blue' is established through experience. A truth of reason on the other hand, is one whose truth can be established without reference to experience. Instead, their truth is decidable by an analysis of the terms involved in the statement. The statement 7+5=12 is a truth of reason. Because truths of reason are not dependent on how experience turned out, they are *always* true and hence *necessarily* true. Arguably, they also do not tell you anything genuinely new about the world, as their truth or otherwise is already contained implicitly in the terms. If I understand the meaning of the symbols 5, 7,12, + and =, i.e. if I understand the framework of number theory, then I can verify that the statement 5+7=12 is true[xxxix].

Consider a further example. We are taught at school that angles in a triangle add up to 180° and this can be proved fairly easily using the technique of walking around the perimeter. But then let's see what happens when we try this on the surface of the earth. Suppose I start at the north pole and travel south. When I get to the equator, I turn 90° to the right and travel a quarter of the way around the equator. I then turn 90° to face north and travel back to the north pole. I then need to turn another 90° to the right in order to face the way I started. So I have now travelled a triangle with internal angles of 90° + 90° + 90° = 270°! I remember thinking this was amazing, when I first thought about this! The 'truth' that angles in a triangle add up to 180° only holds within the framework of Euclidian geometry, the geometry of flat surfaces. When you move on to curved surfaces the rules of the game change and different truths hold. So when discussing truths of reason, it is import to be aware of the framework within which we are working. In everyday life, we can make statements like 7+5=12 without needing to qualify this and add on the end 'within the framework of number theory'. It is taken as a given that we are using the standard framework of number theory. But it is important to be aware that this caveat is lurking in the background.

What about empirical statements though? These are propositions that say something about the world e.g. the earth has only one moon. The status of truths of fact are harder to decide because we need to understand both the meaning of the terms and whether or not the state of affairs described actually obtains. For truths of reason, we are discussing abstract structures or well-defined terms, such as in the statement 'all bachelors are unmarried', which means that there is no uncertainty in the system and that therefore the truth of any such statement is fully decidable in principle[xl]. This is because an abstract structure has both finite complexity and has a structure that is known and therefore unambiguous.

Let's consider the question of whether an object in the sky is an aeroplane. To say 'Yes, the thing up there is a plane' is not a statement whose truth can be decided by an analysis of the terms alone. We need to consider the sense data we are receiving. We noted that the object was white with sticky out bits at the sides and decided that the model that best fit this data was that the object is an aeroplane. To see this more clearly, consider putting your hand inside a bag and being asked to identify something inside by touch alone. Maybe it's something quite hard, long and thin. Maybe it's smooth on the wider long sides, but rough on the narrower long sides – it feels like there are lots of little holes on these narrow sides. Suddenly, you realise it is a harmonica![30] Once you apply the harmonica model, the rest of the sense impressions you get all make sense.

We can comment about our sense impressions, but it is only when we fit a model to it that we get something meaningful that we can assess for truth, such as 'the object in the bag is a harmonica'. Even just a basic statement about the world such as 'I see a white patch' needs a model of some kind – we need to know what we mean by 'white'.

So both truths of reason and truths of fact are decidable only once we understand the model, or framework, within which they are expressed. This raises the question of how we know whether the model is 'true' – whether the model correctly models independent reality. However, as we

[30] This example is taken from 'Why red doesn't sound like a bell' by J. Kevin O'Regan

have covered extensively, it serves no purpose to ask if a model is a 'true' representation of independent reality, because we cannot know anything about the Superunknowable. The only thing we could assess a particular model against is a wider, or higher level model. Rather than assessing models as 'true' or 'false', we instead consider whether they are useful or appropriate. Models are appropriate if they allow you to make good sense of the incoming data, or inappropriate if they lead to confusion. The purpose of this book is to argue that the confusion about the existence or otherwise of God would be greatly reduced if a kind of 'Copernican Revolution' transformed the relationship of Truth and Belief. Because in our 'Common Sense' way of thinking, belief is subject to truth. Whether you are right or wrong in believing in God depends on the truth of whether or not God exists. But now we have seen that things can make much more sense if you look at them the other way around. Whether or not it is true to say that God exists depends on which model you believe in – on the framework you are using to make sense of the world.

So when asking whether a statement is true, the first response might be 'within what framework?' A statement involves language. Language involves concepts. Concepts only have meaning within a framework. Do angles in a triangle add up to 180°? Well within what framework? Is light a wave? In the framework of Maxwell's theory of electro-magnetism, yes, in the framework of quantum mechanics, no. Does God exist? Within what framework? Within the framework of Christianity, yes, within the framework of atheism, no. 'Yes, but which is true, Christianity or atheism?'. Christianity and atheist are not statements that could be true or false. They are models that can be useful or not useful.

Anything Goes?

If all this feels somewhat disorientating, then perhaps this is not surprising. 'Tell me your truth', said TV host Oprah Winfrey to princess Meghan Markle in their famous 2021 interview, provoking some comment. Is 'the truth' now anything you want it to be? This is perhaps the main reason why we cling to the idea that there must be something concrete behind the world of phenomena. It is to ground our perceptions to something objective that we can all agree on.

And this hasn't changed. Our experiences behave in certain ways which allow the application of a structure. And this means that although our understanding of it is only a model, there can be good models and bad models. A good model will help us make sense of our experiences, whereas a bad model leads to confusion. So, for example, a model that says pigs can fly will lead to confusion when it is observed that pigs don't fly. This means that when we say 'Anything Goes' in terms of your metaphysical model of the Superunknowable, there is an important caveat, namely that it must be an appropriate model – it must be consistent with our experiences. It's a bit like trying to fit one of those elasticated bedsheets over the mattress. You can choose whatever colour or texture of bedsheet you like, but the bedsheet must fit the mattress.

Let's suppose that I say God exists, and I insist that I am right, because this is the case in my model – in the framework I use to make sense of my experiences. However, if you say God does not exist, you might think you are right for the same reason – how do we resolve this? My God governs my world and so looks after the you that is in my world, *even though* for you, there might not be a God. There is no contradiction here, because the truth of God's existence is followed by a 'for me' – we are using different models to explain the same phenomena. The upshot of this is that God is *personal*. The good news is that irrespective of whether or not you have a God, no-one has any grounds to say that you are wrong. The trade-off is that you have to respect other people's realities in that you have no grounds for imposing your God on others.

Living with Contradiction

On 22 January 2017, then Councillor to U.S. President Trump, Kellyanne Conway, coined the now notorious phrase 'Alternative Facts'. The TV news anchor had challenged Ms Conway to justify why the president's spokesperson had been instructed to provide falsehoods about the size of the crowd attending Trump's inauguration ceremony. Ms Conway responded that the press secretary had merely given 'alternative facts'. The TV news anchor was left in the bizarre situation of having to point out that "'alternative facts' are not facts. They are falsehoods."[xli]

Yet haven't our investigations so far shown that things are not that simple? The idea that there is a single set of facts about the world relies on an independent reality that can be split up into individual elements (facts), that are the same for all of us. We have now seen that this is impossible. God may exist for me but not for you, because what is a feature of my model may not be a feature of yours. So what is stopping us from extending this concept to anything? If I say Trump's inauguration crowd was the biggest ever, then that was the case in the way I model my experiences and you are in no position to challenge that. That is my truth. You are not me and you experience reality differently to the way I experience it.

Is it not an unavoidable consequence of the Anything Goes school, that whatever appears true to me *is* true because that is how I model it? I cannot be wrong about anything. We discussed in chapter 11 how language provides us with the capacity to be wrong, even under the Anything Goes School of Metaphysics. The reason why we can't just decide that whatever we would like to be true is actually true is that we do not have full sight of what we will experience in the future. Our experiences are continually changing, but not all of these changes are a result of our own volition. We don't know what will happen next. It is outside our control. And therefore as much as we might want it to be hot and sunny tomorrow, it might rain. We cannot just decide that it is not raining and lo and behold, it stops raining. If the aeroplane flaps its wings, then it is not an aeroplane. Our models need to be consistent with our experiences, otherwise our model is not appropriate. We may or may not think that there is or isn't a God based on our experiences of the world to date. This is different to insisting that it is not raining, even though there is water coming out the sky and we are getting wet. It is important to remember Wittgenstein's point that words mean what they are used to mean. If you are experiencing water coming out the sky then it *is* raining by definition. In order for the 'under the Anything Goes approach, Truth is whatever you want it to be' accusation to stick, we would need to be able to stop the water coming out the sky just by willing it.

What about a situation where someone else's model fits the data, but we would still view the model as clearly wrong under normal circumstances? For example, what if someone did believe that pigs can fly? Following the logic of what we have discussed so far, it could be argued that for this person, because the model is all there is, it is true under their framework that pigs can fly. When they then throw a pig out the window and it doesn't fly, we imagine this person will adjust their model accordingly and it will no longer be true for them that pigs can fly. Obviously, it seems ridiculous to take the claim that pigs can fly seriously, but remember the inductivist turkey. Even though this would raise serious questions about everything else we think we know about how our experiences behave, who can say for sure that one day a pig might not fly?

The second question is how to reconcile these two different 'truths'? Surely pigs either can fly or they cannot; we can't both be right? But this is a scientific realist way of thinking. As in the aeroplane/bird/binoculars scenario described above, when models collide here, one of us will be forced to change our model. When push comes to shove and the pig is observed not to fly, our believer is likely going to accept that pigs never could fly and that he was previously in error, rather than that pigs have stopped flying or that it is only *this* pig that cannot fly. This process is no different in practice to the way disagreements are resolved under the common-sense picture. Both before and after the Copernican revolution, people have their different beliefs. When these beliefs come into conflict, efforts are made to resolve the issue based on the incoming data from the common world that we both experience. This results in a new shared belief. The Copernican revolution between truth and belief therefore doesn't impact how we resolve disagreements about Truths of Fact at the everyday level. It does however help us harmonise disagreements about the existence of God, where the incoming data cannot assist in resolving different views.

Of course, it may be that our protagonist does *not* accept that they were in error previously and insists that pigs used to fly. What then? We might start by pointing out that due to pig aerodynamics; the lack of wings etc., it is impossible for pigs to fly or at least contradictory to everything else we think we know about the world. Perhaps our protagonist believes that God has given certain pigs secret powers of flight where wings are not needed. But perhaps our protagonist is comfortable with pigs flying and does not need a reason for how this is possible. Perhaps they accept that pigs are round, heavy, have no wings and yet still believes that they fly, as a brute fact with no explanation. What then? What if you insist on believing something that is logically impossible? Are we still saying that under the Anything Goes approach it is true, even though logically, it cannot possibly be? Perhaps a slightly less provocative way of phrasing the question would be 'Is it reasonable to assert that this is the way things are for me, even though the model I am using to make sense of it contains a contradiction?'

Let's say our protagonist accepts that all men are mortal. And they accept that Socrates is a man. But perhaps they refuse to accept that Socrates is mortal.

"But if you accept that all men are mortal, then if Socrates is a man, then it *must* be the case that he is mortal. He is a man, so he is one of those that is mortal, given that, without exception, all men, and so this includes Socrates, who is, as we have just said, a man, are mortal. Logically, you have to accept it."

"No, I don't accept it. I disagree. Who says I have to accept it and what right do they have to tell me what I have to accept?"

Of course, not all Truths of Reason are so easily established. Famously, Fermat's Last Theorem, which states that there are no three positive integers a, b, and c that satisfy the equation $a^n + b^n = c^n$ for any integer value of n greater than 2, was stated by French mathematician Pierre de Fermat in 1637, but only shown to be true by English mathematician Andrew Wiles in 1995[xlii]. Is there a problem with a failure to recognise Truths of Reason, which we have seen are necessarily and always true (as far as logic and mathematics are concerned)? One issue with a failure to recognise Truths of Reason is that it can result is disagreements between people. These disagreements are resolvable in principle, at least under the terms dictated by logic and mathematics, given the abstract and finite nature of the system under contention. The interesting cases are those where the model contains an inconsistency that is not readily apparent. We might call these 'latent inconsistencies', in contrast to the patently obvious inconsistency involving Socrates above. However, these abstract structures form more than just points of academic debate – they form the basis of the models we use to make sense of the world. We fit the incoming data to these models and as such there are consequences for the establishment of Truths of Fact. Our user may be using an inconsistent model to navigate the world quite happily until a situation occurs that brings the inconsistency to light. If I agree a price of £40, hand over a £50 note and then expect £20 change, this is going to cause me problems. And we have already examined the consequences of a reliance on the model of solipsism. If I know it takes me five minutes to get to the station and but leave at 0658 thinking I can make the 0700 train, then I will be disappointed. What went wrong? My model said I could make the train, so it was true that I could make the train. Except that it wasn't. It turns out that my model did not describe the behaviour of my experience accurately enough to be useful.

Who can be sure that none of the models that we use in the 21st century contain a latent inconsistency that will become apparent in future and cause problems? We can say that such models are problematic and incoherent. We can say that once these problems emerge into the light of day, the models will likely be rejected as inappropriate as a description of how things are for me. Can we say they are 'wrong'? Under the scientific realist picture, it might be argued that while a particular coherent model may or may not be a true description of how independent reality is structured, an incoherent model cannot possibly be true. If independent reality is structured in a certain way, then if the model of it is incoherent then at least some part of it must be wrong[31]. Under the Anything Goes

---

[31] Although it could perhaps be argued that even this is not clear cut. We have already seen that nature behaves in ways that can appear contradictory (is light a wave or a particle?), and anyway, as we have seen in chapter 8, it is possibly incoherent to claim that the structure of reality, as it is independently of our conception of it, can make sense to us.

methodology however, we are not looking for a correspondence between the structure of the model and the structure of independent reality and so it is not really appropriate to characterise models as right or wrong. They just are what they are – we are interested in whether they are useful. So instead, it is perhaps more accurate to describe reliance on a model that contains latent inconsistencies as problematic and reliance on models that contain patent inconsistencies as perverse.

So now we come to disagreements about the existence of God. Unlike with flying pigs and birds/aeroplanes, this situation cannot be resolved by an appeal to the data provided by our shared world. Both the believer and unbeliever are using a model which for them, fits the data. But following the proposed Copernican revolution reversing the relationship of truth and belief, there is no paradox or inconsistency that needs resolving. I respect that the metaphysics you use to make sense of your experiences is different from the model I use to make sense of mine, and due to the lack of information about the Superunknowable, to the extent that both models are consistent with our experiences, there are no grounds for claiming that one is more valid than the other.

*

So far, I've concentrated on tackling perhaps the principle objection to what I have called the 'Anything Goes' approach. But there are other possible objections. Let's now take a quick look at each of these in turn.

The Anything Goes approach is incoherent

It might be alleged that the Rob Hamilton 'Anything Goes' school of metaphysics is incoherent and contains a paradox at its heart. If, for each of us, any model you have faith in speaks the truth, what if, for you, the model that you have faith in is 'It is not the case that for each of us, the model you have faith in speaks the truth' or 'Only my model speaks the truth'? This might be a tempting intellectual avenue for your hardliners, who struggle to accept those with views that differ from their own.

The paradox is resolved when you appreciate that the 'Anything Goes' concept applies only to substantive models of reality – so models that say something about the nature of reality – for example 'There is a God' or 'Space is three dimensional'. The Anything Goes School of Metaphysics says "It's all just models, so pick one that works for you". The alternative to the Anything Goes approach is one that says "It's not all models" – one that asserts that the objects in my understanding of the world around me really exist, independently of my view on it. Or in other words, forms of scientific realism. So taking the first avenue, to state 'It is not the case that for each of us, the model you have faith in speaks the truth' is to advocate for scientific realism. It is not a statement made within the Anything Goes framework and therefore it is not subject to the idea that believing it to be true, makes it true for the believer.

So once it is realised that the Anything Goes framework is different to the kinds of metaphysical models we have been talking about, it can be seen that there can be no self-referencing. The Anything Goes concept is a framework for metaphysical models, but is not one itself. Instead, the Anything Goes idea makes no claims about the substantive nature of the world. Instead it is a kind of meta-metaphysics, providing the ground for possible metaphysical models upon which to base our experiences.

Let's move on to the second avenue for the hardliner, namely that of stating that 'Only my model speaks the truth'. A few moments' reflection shows that this is scientific realism in disguise. Models cannot be true or false; they are either useful or not useful. And in the final analysis, only you can know what models works best for you. So I can say that 'In my world, God looks after everyone, including you', but commenting on what is the case for you in your world, is out of bounds for me. To say otherwise, is to say that the form of your world is a result of more than just how you model it – such claims are realist and unjustifiable.

The Anything Goes approach is arrogant

God is omnipotent, awe-inspiring and beyond the comprehension of the human mind, or so it is often claimed. It is the height of arrogance therefore, to assert that some human framework provides the overarching truth about Reality and then look to insert God into a pigeon-hole within this framework. Maybe so. On the line of thinking exemplified in Reformed Epistemology, our belief systems and frameworks should be assessed against the backdrop of God, not the other way around. This is the kind of criticism employed by theologians such as Cornelius Van Til[xliii], who says

'A God of whom it is possible to ask intelligently whether he exists is not the God of Scripture. The God of Scripture is back of all possible eventuation in the space-time world. It is an insult to this God to argue for his possible existence'

This tactic is most commonly employed when people are seeking to counter the challenge that there is no proof of God's existence. Note that this is an argument between realists of different stripes. The reformed epistemologist insists that God exists for everyone as a starting point – the is no qualification that this might only be the case from your own perspective, which is why the position is a realist one. As noted previously, in Reformed Epistemology, experience of God is basic, which means that it is taken as given and does not stand in need of explanation. It is the starting point for all our other judgements. Of course, this immediately raises the question, 'if you have God as your basic starting point, why can I not have something else as my basic starting point?', such as 'I see a white patch'. Such an experience would appear to be more basic than that of an unnecessary entity with arbitrary characteristics. The 20th Century American philosopher Alvin Platinga seeks to draw an equivalence with 'I see white', by arguing that a statement like 'I hear God' is basic. However, we can quickly see that this is a false equivalence, as God is a complex idea, rather than an unprocessed sense impression. 'I see white' is to 'I see a bird' as 'I hear a voice' is to 'I hear God'. When inferring that what we are hearing is God, we are fitting a model. So the claim that God is basic falls apart.

This analysis is unlikely to persuade Reformed Epistemologists however, and given everything we have discussed, we have to accept that people are free to reject the Anything Goes framework, if they find it objectionable. However, in order for any such rejection to have substance and therefore be persuasive, critics would need to identify problems with the reasoning or propose a more useful or satisfying way of looking at things. Otherwise, it might seem like just closing your eyes with your fingers in your ears, like our friend who refused to accept that Socrates is mortal.

To assuage those who may still have concerns that the Anything Goes approach diminishes God's status in some way, it might be argued that God as he makes himself known to us, is different to the mysterious and unfathomable God as he is in himself. It could perhaps be suggested that God in his full majesty, is indeed beyond the comprehension of the human mind. The Anything Goes framework provides a way of helping us understand God as he might appear to us.

The Anything Goes approach is hypocritical

Finally, we might ask whether, even if it is not paradoxical, can the Anything Goes approach be criticised as hypocritical? The Anything Goes approach castigates other religious and metaphysical systems for claiming that they are the only true religion, but is this not exactly what the Anything Goes approach claims for itself? But perhaps we should leave that as an interesting exam question, rather than get bogged down fighting that battle here!

Chapter 13

13. Virtual Reality

We are now nearing the end of our investigation. We have thoroughly investigated the question of whether or not God exists and we have assuaged any worries that may have arisen regarding the implications of the Anything Goes approach for broader questions of existence and the possibility of error in everyday life. We may have resolved the God confusion, but before we close, let's run through how the Anything Goes approach might be applied when considering the existence of a few other entities. We might start with something uncontroversial, the existence of which we all accept, and go from there.

Animals in the Wild

Lovers of nature understandably get very excited when they see a rare breed of animal whilst out walking in the hills or taking a boat trip. As biodiversity continues to fall, perhaps it is natural that we think about how much longer these creatures will continue to exist in their traditional haunts. To take Scotland as an example, historical records indicate that in centuries gone by, wolves existed in the wild. Official documents suggest that the last wolf was killed in 1680, but there are reports of wolves surviving through to the 18th or even 19th centuries. Could wolves exist in the wild in Scotland today? Let's see how the Anything Goes approach handles this. We might first imagine the simple case of a wolf in a cage in front of us. We could see such a wolf. The incoming data would fit the model of a wolf. Based on what we have discussed, it would be straightforward to say that that there was a wolf in the cage. That this wolf exists. Now what about the more general question of wild wolves? Under the common-sense picture, we would expect the answer to be 'no', as a matter of fact.

Now one might think *prima facie* that under the Anything Goes framework, if I believe that there are wild wolves in Scotland, then, given that the map is the territory, this means that it is true that there are wild wolves in Scotland, at least for me. But perhaps the situation is a little more nuanced than this. I remember the bird/aeroplane fiasco, and I am wary about being too definite in my beliefs, aware that future data may falsify what I currently believe to be the case. Firstly, one might ask, *why* do I believe that there are wild wolves in Scotland? Have I seen one? If I have seen one, I need to be mindful that I could have been mistaken, like when I thought the bird was an aeroplane. Or perhaps, I just love wolves, for their wild and romantic nature. The Scottish Highlands are also wild and romantic, so I would really love it if there were wild wolves in some remote Highland glens and this makes me want to believe that there are. Anything Goes methodology gives me a licence to insist that anything I like is true, as long as the data can't disprove it – brilliant! However I must ask myself, do I really *believe* that there are wild wolves in Scotland? We noted when discussing Pascal's wager that you cannot just choose what to believe, in the way that you might choose between having a cup of tea or coffee. Your beliefs might be better thought of as your expectations about the world based on your past experiences – they are not fully under your control. I need to weigh my desire for there to be wild wolves in Scotland and any past sightings against my understanding that if there really were wild wolves in Scotland, they would be preying on deer or sheep and this would likely attract the attention of crofters and landowners and result in some publicity.

So perhaps, with a more sober mindset, I believe that there are no wild wolves in Scotland. Does this mean that under the Anything Goes approach that this is definitely true? Under the common-sense picture, although we believe there are no wild wolves in Scotland, the possibility remains that this is wrong and there are a small number deep in the Caledonian Forest, eking out an existence beyond the seemingly unstoppable encroachment of humanity. But if the Map is the Territory, does this mean that under the Anything Goes approach, there is zero chance of there being wild wolves in Scotland, simply because I believe this to be the case? Again, this is an oversimplification. What I actually believe is that it is *unlikely* that there are wild wolves in Scotland, but not impossible. We can't say for sure either way, until we have inspected every square meter of land in Scotland simultaneously, and considered whether or not it contains a wolf. While this may be impossible in practice, it is possible in principle. Scotland and wolves are part of my model of the Superunknowable. To understand whether or not there are wild wolves in Scotland, I would need to inspect a very large part of my model, and consider a large number of data points all at once, which I cannot do. Imagine getting out your 1:25,000 scale maps of Scotland and counting how many triangulation pillars (aka trig points) there are.

If I want my model of reality to be internally consistent, which I do if I want it to be useful, then I will not be making stand alone assertions about whether there are or are not wolves in Scotland as a brute fact, with no context or consideration for my other beliefs about the world. Rather, the question of whether there are wolves in Scotland is a question about the content of my model, rather than its form. We are now in a position to respond to the charge at the beginning of Part III that the Anything Goes approach destroys the gap between what is, and what can be known. The

Anything Goes approach asks us to select a metaphysical framework that allows us to model our experiences in an acceptable way. This framework may or may not include God. However, just having discovered an acceptable model does not put us in a position of having a God's eye view of our model – we cannot contemplate the whole map at once. What, in the common-sense picture, is us navigating the world, is in the Anything Goes framework us moving around on our map – just like if you are lost in the fog and using GPS navigation. Your world becomes the blue dot moving around the screen. You only see the part of the map that's on the screen at any one time. There are new places to explore, new experiences that will happen; having a model of independent reality does not mean we suddenly know everything. The situation with God is different, as future data cannot falsify my model, even in principle, even after I die. God is part of the framework, rather than the content.

Ghosts, Dragons and Father Christmas

If it is possible that there are wild wolves hiding out in some remote corner of the country, then is it also possible that there be dragons hidden away from us as well[32]? As with the wild wolves question, we know what a dragon is and we can also note that it is subject to the 'discoverable in principle' criterion. We could, in principle, inspect every square metre of land in the world, every cubic metre above and below ground and in the sea, and consider whether or not it contains a dragon. This suggests that question of whether dragons actually exist is about the content of our maps, rather than the form. Obviously, the important difference when considering dragons, as opposed to wolves, is that we have never actually *seen* a dragon. The evidence in favour of there being no such things as dragons seems pretty overwhelming.

What about ghosts? Well, first, what are ghosts, exactly? Are they subject to the 'discoverable in principle' criterion? If they exist, could you corner one, and say 'Aha! I see you exist!'. Or do they fade in and out of existence at whim or based on certain triggers, like the anniversary of someone's

---

[32] We are considering mythical fire-breathing dragons here, rather than your common or garden Komodo dragon.

death? Can everybody see ghosts, or is it only certain people with a spiritual sensitivity? If ghosts can fade in and out of existence and are not made of anything physical, then we are moving away from discussing the content of our maps and more considering the map's form – the idea that it is possible for things to come into and out of existence. If you believe in the supernatural and these concepts provide the best explanation for the events that you experience, then who is to tell you that you are wrong? Of course, they may confront you with awkward questions like 'How does the spirit subsist after death? What are ghosts made of? What is ectoplasm, exactly?' to try to convince you that mundane explanations for any apparent paranormal activity are more appropriate. But then, the religious have long had to wrestle with difficult questions like 'If God is good, why are there natural disasters?' and the Problem of Evil, noted previously.

Can we apply the same line of reasoning to dragons? If I insist that dragons exists because I believe in them, then am I right? Again, if I want my model of reality to be internally consistent, then I will not be making stand alone assertions about whether dragons exist as a brute fact, with no context or consideration for my other beliefs about the world. The evidence I have seen suggests there are no dragons. We could also appeal to Occam's Razor, and note that while the existence of dragons may appeal to my sense of romance and whimsy, a model including dragons lacks substance in that it doesn't help with our understanding of the world.

*

Many children around the world, particularly in the West, believe in Father Christmas. They are told that if they well-behaved throughout the year, then they will wake up on Christmas morning to find that Father Christmas has left them presents during the night. And lo, this does come to pass. These sweet children have no reason to doubt the explanation provided by their ever-loving parents and this theory is supported by the evidence. Given that the Map is the Territory, this theory must therefore be true. These conniving and underhand parents have a different explanation, however. They know very well, that it was them that sneaked the presents in while the children were asleep. How do we reconcile these two different versions of the Truth?

By now, I expect we all know what is coming. Given that we can have no knowledge of the Superunknowable, there is no single version of The Truth. The child's explanation is just as true within the context of the child's model of reality as the parents' explanation is within *their* model. But then the child gets a bit older. They hear whispers in the school playground that really it's your parents and perhaps this leads to a confrontation, where the two worlds collide and the truth of the Father Christmas myth is discussed between parent and child. The game is up. The parents confess that it was them all along. As with when the aeroplane started to flap its wings, there is now a decision to be made[33]. Does the child believe that at that moment, Father Christmas stopped existing, or does the child now believe that he never existed? Which is a better fit to the data and is a more useful model for the future? Given that we are all brought up with the common-sense picture, this is not even a conscious decision, but it is worth understanding that in principle there are these two paths that can be followed, in order to understand how the Anything Goes framework fits in with everyday life.

The revelation that Father Christmas doesn't exist is even more dramatic than merely saying 'everything I thought I knew was wrong'. In fact, given that the Map is the Territory, accepting a new model means that the child's world has fundamentally changed. It is not just what you see that is changing, but how you see it. The framework changes, rather than just the content. To say, 'In that moment, my whole world changed' is literally true.

The Eucharist

In chapter 2, I introduced the anti-realist approach to religion and noted that it was based on the coherence theory of truth. This approach rejects the idea that true statements correspond with facts about the world and

[33] We could also address another extreme possibility, namely that the child refuses to accept the parents' explanation and continues to believe in Father Christmas.

instead argues that statements can be considered true if they cohere with other statements within the belief system. We noted that statements such as 'God exists' and 'Mary was a virgin' are considered to be true by virtue of being accepted as such within the community. Given what we now know about the impossibility of understanding the structure of the Superunknowable (if it even exists), can we now consider this approach to be more credible than perhaps we gave it credit for at the start of the book?

We also noted in the previous chapter that one of the reasons why the truth cannot be just whatever we want it to be is that our beliefs need to be in line with our experiences. What do our experiences teach us about the idea of walking on water? If we don't have a God or accept the idea of the supernatural, then we are unlikely to accept the idea that Jesus walked on water, at least without it having been some kind of trick. On the other hand, if we do have a God and recognise that he acts in the world, then we may accept this as possible in principle. What about if your God is not the Christian God, or if your God is the 'thin' God of the Epicureans that does not act in the world?

Another of the ideas accepted as true in anti-realist communities is that wine is transubstantiated into the blood of Christ at communion. Is this belief in line with our experiences? Anti-realists would, of course, accept that if the transubstantiated wine was taken to the lab and subjected to testing, the results would show that it was wine, rather than blood. 'For a blunder, that's too big', as Wittgenstein put it. Nonetheless, for the anti-realist, it is true that the transubstantiated wine *is* the blood of Christ, rather than the whole process merely being metaphorical i.e. a symbolic ritual. For this to make sense, we therefore need theologians to come up with a clever way of looking at things in order for this not to be a contradiction of the lab test results. Although scientific testing demonstrates that physically, the red liquid is still wine, a different kind of transformation has occurred resulting in the wine becoming the blood of Christ. As we saw when discussing ghosts above, this assertion moves the nature of the red liquid away from being part of the content of the map, where it can be subject to enquiry, and onto it being part of the form of the map; our map states that things can change in a way that is neither physical, nor metaphorical.

The anti-realist position might therefore be viewed as quite an extreme position within the Anything Goes framework. Up to now, we have been considering those features of our map such as God and other minds, which are largely outside the domain of scientific enquiry. But under anti-realism, we encroach upon the territory of science. We are making claims about the nature of liquids and humans, where scientific enquiry can give us an answer. If anti-realism wants to insist on different answers and avoid the charge of Fictionalism, we need some imaginative linguistic gymnastics, if not downright double-speak. This can lead to problems. In chapter 12, we noted that Anything Goes methodology leads to a map that is intensely personal. The onus is on each of us to find a map that works for us. Anti-realism, on the other hand, stresses the importance of community. If testing reveals the liquid to be wine, then we need a community to reinforce the idea that it is also the blood of Christ. One consequence of this might be that truths are somewhat arbitrary. For example, under what circumstances can transubstantiation occur? Who can do it? Must it take place within a church? It might also be noted that you end up delegating a significant amount of power over your life to a third party. If we cannot test our beliefs against experience, we are bound to community leaders such as the magisterium in Rome as arbiters of truth. Anti-realists can of course counter by pointing out that everyone lives in a community of one kind or other and all belief systems will inevitably include a degree of dogma whether you are aware of it or not. As we have been exploring throughout this book.

The Matrix Reloaded

We spoke earlier about Descartes' concern that everything we experience may not be real and how this scenario was updated in the 1999 film 'The Matrix', where Descartes' evil demon is reincarnated in the form of an all-powerful artificial intelligence network. A similar scenario was also considered by 20th Century philosopher Hilary Putnam in his 'brain in a vat' thought experiment. In Putnam's scenario, an evil scientist removes someone's brain, but keeps it alive in a vat of nutrients and stimulates it artificially, such that the mind inside the brain still believes that it is fully human; with a fully human body, living in a normal world.

Putnam's thought experiment provoked some debate – Putnam's own position being that this worry need not concern anyone. He used a referentialist argument, to try to show that a brain in vat would not be able to think 'maybe I am a brain in a vat'[xliv]. However critics of this argument, as well as criticising its referentialist underpinnings, have pointed out that even if you accept this argument, the fact that you can't think something doesn't mean that the thing you can't think can't be true. An ant might not be able to think "I'm an ant" but that doesn't mean it's not an ant. Debate on this matter continued.

Now armed with the understanding we have built up, we can approach this problem applying Anything Goes methodology – we immediately see that the scenario as constructed by Putnam is problematic. In the thought experiment, there is firstly the brain's perspective and secondly the actual reality of the situation. But as we have discussed at length, it makes no sense to talk about a single objective reality. There are only points of view of the various observers. So we will have to refine the thought experiment slightly and ask "Could it be, that while I see myself as a normal human being, someone else sees me as a brain in a vat and is controlling my experiences?"

This is perhaps slightly less disturbing, as there are no grounds to believe that their perspective on reality is ontologically superior to my own; that is to say that there is no reason to think that their viewpoint is any 'more real' than my own. "Sounds like a 'you' problem", as my niece might say. However, this is more than just a semantic shift. The first question this raises is, without being able to point to a common structured underlying reality, what reason do we have to accept the premise that the brain the scientist is manipulating has anything to do with the 'me' who believes he is a normal human? The scientist twiddles some dials and sends some signals to the brain – how does he know that the consciousness in the brain is experiencing what the scientist expects them to be experiencing or even that there is a consciousness in there at all? This brings us back to the problem of other minds which we will come on to shortly.

Now the consciousness in the brain is blissfully unaware that it is the scientist who is providing the inputs that feed into his experiences. Of course, you don't need to be an evil scientist to have some control over inputs into someone's experiences without their knowledge. I can do this, for example, by hiding your car keys. One might object that the difference is that by hiding the car keys, I am changing their experience, rather than giving them a fake experience. But since the 'real world' is unknowable, it doesn't really make sense to talk about a 'fake' experience. We choose to view the rubber hand as the 'fake' experience only for consistency with our wider model. Instead of hiding their car keys, I could bash them over their head so they lose their memory and then clamp a virtual reality headset on them. They are still having experiences based on an external input. The fact that they are not getting input from the world outside the headset is no different from you or I not getting input from some location that is out of sight. The evil scientist scenario is just a rather extreme version of someone manipulating the things you experience without your knowledge.

Notwithstanding these observations, our primary concern remains. It remains possible that the model of the universe that I live by will fail. In the film 'The Matrix', the main character experiences a number of bizarre and seemingly impossible events, which prompt him to question the appropriateness of his model. And who can say that instead of the sun rising tomorrow, as I expect, instead there will be nothing but blackness? At that point, I may conclude that a more appropriate model is that an evil scientist has just pulled the plug. Ultimately, the brain-in-a-vat thought experiment just transposes to the Inductivist Turkey problem discussed previously. However well we think we understand the world around us, the future always has the potential to surprise us.

*

In the examples above, I've tried to show that not only does Anything Goes methodology fit in perfect naturally with everyday life, but that it helps us resolve a number of conundrums in addition to the question of whether God exists. In the next chapter, I'll explore what happens when we apply this method to another high profile issue of our time – that of consciousness. Could artificial intelligence systems ever attain consciousness for example? Let's have a look.

Chapter 14

14. What is Consciousness?

I'm sure that at some point in our lives, we have all wondered what it would be like to step into someone else's shoes and see the world from a different perspective. 'Try looking at things from their point of view' is a common piece of advice whenever disagreements arise, and conflicts need to be resolved. But what if the world doesn't actually contain any other points of view? What if everyone you meet, while behaving like a normal human being, is actually just an automaton – a zombie – with no thoughts and feelings of their own? How could we ever know if this is the case? This is the 'problem of other minds' touched on earlier, when we were discussing solipsism.

As noted when we considered solipsists, we don't tend to come across people in real life who don't believe that other people have minds of their own. Holding such a view must make the world a very lonely place. Each person they meet is not considered to be a real person. Each person is not human. They don't have any feelings that need to be taken into account, when interacting with them. They can't be upset. They don't feel pain. There is no point in treating them with any respect. However, they behave as if they are human. This sounds like a recipe for disaster and we can image that such an outlook would land you either in prison or in a psychiatric hospital in short order!

Although this is an interesting question for philosophers, it is perhaps not one that really worries most of us. Throughout life, I encounter people who look like me, walk, talk and act like me, and so it is natural to assume that they must be conscious beings, just like me. They look like me – they have the same number of eyes, ears and limbs as me. They behave like me – If I stub my toe, it hurts and I cry out in pain. If they stub their toe, I see them cry out in pain and I assume it must have hurt them too. As the saying goes, if it looks like a duck, swims like a duck and quacks like a duck, then it probably is a duck. This is known as the argument from analogy[xlv]. It sounds crazy to imagine that amongst the multitude of people you interact with every day, you might be the only one that is actually a conscious thinking being. With seven billion people on the planet, what are the chances that you are the only one with a mind?[34] At this point some people like to make reference to the anthropic principle and point out that if there was only one conscious mind on the planet, and all the rest were zombies, the chances of it being you who is the conscious mind is 100% guaranteed! This is because it is not possible for a zombie to think 'Am I a zombie?' Given that you are able to ask the question, you must have a conscious mind. However, this still doesn't explain how we came to have a situation with seven billion people on the planet, with only one of them being conscious.

So we are generally happy to take it as a given that we are all conscious thinking beings. Where we start to move onto shakier ground is in the consideration of non-human consciousness. Are all animals conscious, for example? The French philosopher René Descartes insisted that all animals are unthinking beings. Should we agree? Is consciousness a black and white, yes or no phenomenon or are there levels of consciousness? We might expect that primates, such as chimpanzees and gorillas for example, have a higher level of awareness of the world around them than insects. Or is the most interesting question the distinction between having some awareness, rather than no awareness, irrespective of how much? This is a particularly topical question at the moment given the recent advances in Artificial Intelligence, with large language models such as

[34] Perhaps 1 in 7 billion?

ChatGPT gaining mainstream use. Could machines or other non-biological systems become conscious? What are the implications for humanity if they can? To help investigate this, it is worth pinning down a bit more precisely what we mean when we say that an entity is conscious. The dictionary describes 'consciousness' as being aware of and responding to one's surroundings; it describes being conscious *of* something as having knowledge of that thing. For our purposes, we are looking at the first definition – consciousness as a point of view or perspective on the world. There seems to be something very binary about such a concept – humans have a perspective on the world around us. Bricks and stones do not. So how does consciousness arise? Presumably before the formation of stars and planets and life, there was nothing in the universe that could be said to be conscious. How does the re-organisation of matter into a particular form result in the emergence of this point of view on the world?

We might turn to modern developments in neuroscience to see if that can help. As we saw in chapter 4, neuroscientists have made significant advances in recent decades in understanding how certain thoughts and feelings are accompanied by different patterns in the brain. By inspecting the brain images of people with certain conditions, scientists are able to associate certain patterns in brain activity with certain features of consciousness. Or are they?

What they are actually doing is identifying correlations between certain patterns of neural activity with certain behaviours. Let's think back to the example of dogs seeing in shades of blue, yellow and grey. We can use our science to speculate what it could be like to be a different person. But as we are not that person, we cannot *know for sure* what it is like, or so it is argued. What sight looks like and what sounds a noise makes are known in philosophical parlance as *qualia*, and it is explaining the nature of such qualia that is the Hard Problem of consciousness. Suppose what you see as blue, I see as green. You look at the sky on a clear day and see that it is blue. I look at the sky and I agree with you that it is blue, because ever since I was a baby I have been taught that when I am looking at the sky on a clear day, the colour I am seeing is called blue. Science does not help us. We both look at the sky on a clear day and light enters our eyes, primarily with a wavelength of around 450 nanometres. The light strikes the retina and a signal is sent to our brains via the optic nerve. At the same time we both have the conscious experience of seeing 'blue'. But who is to say that we are having the same experience? This is different to the dog example discussed previously because, with dogs the biology and behaviour are different. With two people, the biology is essentially the same. The point is that just because the physical conditions are the same, how do we know if this results in the same experience?

From a scientific realist perspective, this looks like a promising line of investigation. After all, if the inputs are the same, and the machinery is the same, then is it not reasonable to conclude that the outputs will be the same? So if our biology is the same and our environment is the same, then we should be able to conclude that we are having the same conscious experience. And that therefore other minds exist. Over the past few decades, neuroscientists have used techniques such as functional magnetic resonance imaging (fMRI) and electroencephalography (EEG) to see which parts of the brain are associated with which stimulae. Experiments with conscious subjects, who provide feedback on when they become aware of certain events, have been conducted to try to understand which areas of the brain are associated with conscious experience in order to try to get us closer to an understanding of how consciousness is generated.

However, how far this argument takes us is unclear. Science is still missing that link that takes us from the physical situation to the experience of consciousness. So it is not clear that our current conscious experience is *caused* by our current brain state. We are still presuming that because it walks like a duck, and quacks like a duck, it must think like a duck. Science is still missing that link that takes us from the physical situation to the experience of consciousness. We might know for example what the physical situation is in the brain when I see a patch of red, but we can't answer why the experience of red that correlates with such and such a brain state is like *this* and not like *that*. This is a problem because humans are not identical and so if I can't link a particular brain state to the way I experience it, then I can't know how differences in brain states translate into different experiences. If a robot sends an urgent alarm signal to HQ, saying that one of its limbs has been severed, does it actually *feel* any pain? This has always been the 'hard' problem of consciousness, right back to Kant asking "What is the ground of the relation of that in us which we call 'representation' to the object?" and beyond. Scientific realists ask 'If the world is like this, and I am like that, then how does the world appear to me?' But they find that when they combine facts about the world with facts about the human, all they get is facts about brain states. This is not to belittle the amazing work that has been undertaken in neuroscience over the past few decades, which has greatly increased our understanding of how we interact with the world around us. But because scientific realists view the objects of our models as the 'real' building blocks of the universe, the ontological status of our experience – the sensation of seeing a red patch, for example – needs some thought. It doesn't have any physical form over and above the structures and firing patterns in the brain and so some materialists find that they've backed themselves into a corner and are left with no choice but to deny that such experiences even exist[xlvi]! To put it another way, if there is genuinely no difference in the behaviour of a human with a mind and a zombie – a human shaped automaton, then then mind can have no influence over the behaviour of the body[35]. Like the pink ghost unicorn, it does not exist for practical purposes. And so, as philosopher and psychologist, Philip Johnson-Laird, put it "Any scientific theory of mind has to treat it as an automaton".

A different approach seems to be required. What we need perhaps, is some kind of transformation algorithm that can take us from the world as it *is*, to the world as it *appears*. A way to switch perspectives from the disembodied camera of facts to the world as you or I experience it. But as we have seen, this transformation cannot start with our scientific models, because our scientific models are *part* of our world of experiences. Remember that they are part of our perspective on the world – they inform the way we see the world. Viewing scientific models as providing objective facts about the world is a realist confusion. As we saw in Chapter 7, any scientific model may be falsified in future, so if it so happens that the world

[35] This leads to the problem of Free Will, which we will come on to shortly.

is structured like our latest models say it is (something we can never know), this would be sheer co-incidence. The required transformation therefore starts from the Superunknowable, which sadly means that such a transformation is impossible. The scientific realist creates for themselves an intractable problem by putting experiences at the end of the explanatory chain, asking 'given the world is like this, why are our experiences like that?' However, the red patch is a basic fact about our experience. Our scientific models are there to give the red patch some meaningful context and help us understand how it behaves. Indeed, scientists such as the renowned physicist Richard Feynmann readily point out that scientific models do not give us the 'why', only the 'what'[xlvii]. As we saw when looking at quantum phenonema, scientific models do no more than make predictions about what experiences we will have next. It is up to us to fill in the 'why' – to interpret these models in a way that we find satisfactory. So I would suggest it is therefore more rational to put the experiences at the beginning and ask 'given our experiences are like this, what is the best way of understanding their behaviour?'.

*

To investigate whether there are other minds, we can consider our aeroplane thought experiment from chapter 10, but apply it to a person. It may be that this person is a conscious human or it may be that they are a zombie – let's see what happens. I can understand the concept of a conscious human – a person with a mind of their own. I look at the person and receive sensory impressions that my brain uses to construct a particular phenomenon. I recognise this phenomenon as a conscious human. Perhaps my perception matches the underlying object which is a conscious human, and so I am correct in identifying the phenomenon a conscious human. Alternatively, perhaps I was mistaken. The sensory impressions actually stemmed from something that should have been interpreted as a zombie, rather than a conscious human.

What is the difference between those two alternatives? In both, we have an independent reality, lying behind the person which is unknowable. Also in both scenarios, the object provokes a phenomenon which is interpreted by the observer as a conscious human. The two alternatives are therefore, in terms of the objective facts, *exactly the same!* The only difference between the two scenarios is that in one case we labelled the unknowable thing in itself a human and in the other we labelled it a zombie. But given that the unknowable thing in itself is, and I may have said this before, unknowable, we have no grounds for distinguishing between the two scenarios. The idea that whether or not a machine is conscious comes down to facts above and beyond what can be determined though scientific enquiry – some kind of 'inner nature' – betrays a confusion regarding what can be known about independent reality.

At this point, it might be tempting to object that there is another difference between the two alternatives. In the first situation, even if we don't understand exactly how consciousness works, there is a mind inside that humanoid, whereas in the second, there isn't. However, this objection is wrong-headed. It is incorrect to think of the thing-in-itself as either a human or a zombie. Both humans and zombies are concepts that make sense to us as humans and so are descriptions of phenomena. It is ill-conceived to ask if there is a 'real someone' looking out of the person we see in front of us, when the person itself only exists as an 'object-for-us'. Think back to the rubber hand. The objects that we deal with are created by our brains. It makes no sense to ask whether such an object has a consciousness independent of that which our brains attribute to it, because the object owes its existence only to the fact that our brains created it. The decision as to whether to view other people as having minds is a metaphysical 'choice', analogous to the decision as to whether there is a god. When we talk about minds, we are talking about the thing that experiences the feelings and determines the courses of action taken by the person. So as long as we can observe the person behaving as a conscious being, it is consistent to conclude that they have minds. Understanding the person as having a mind is the best way of understanding its behaviour, and, as the map is the territory, this is *just as true* as the person having arms and legs and the aeroplane being made of atoms. We cannot know the person from the disembodied camera perspective, 'as they are in themselves'. But we do know that the person, as it is experienced by us, has arms, legs and a mind. We would only have occasion to doubt the person has a mind if it starts behaving inconsistently with this idea.

But what if the humanoid only *appears* to be making free choices? To see if they really have a mind, we need to get inside their heads. To which I can reply, well what if the aeroplane only *appears* to be made of atoms? To see what it's actually made of, I need to get past appearances and see the thing in itself. We can only go on the information available based on our point of view. To ask to get 'inside their head' is to ask a question about the superunknowable, which is unanswerable and may not even make any sense. Scientist have tried to look behind the scenes and get inside people's heads and all they found was brain goo. Anything Goes methodology says we shouldn't be surprised by this – the difference between a conscious human and a zombie is metaphysical.

Is this explanation satisfactory? We might be left with the nagging worry that if all objects are just hallucinations created by our brains, then none of the people that we interact with are real people and so the idea that they have minds of their own is just an illusion. This is not the case. Your brain's model is not just a sensory model of how things look, sound and feel. It is a model of how things *are*. *All* the world is models. It is no crazier to think of objects created by your brain as having minds of their own than it is to think of you yourself having a mind of your own. Remember that the idea that there is a you, (distinct from the objects that you think about), is part of the model. Remember when we said that the Superunknowable cannot be divided into the part that is you and the part that is not you? The idea of a thinking 'you' is just as much a part of your model as other thinking objects. So Descartes was subtly, but importantly, wrong with idea that you are ontologically superior to the objects you think about. Kant, on the other hand, saw that subject and object make one another possible. And so the object having a mind is one of its properties, no different to it having a certain size or colour. It's all part of how we understand our experience.

To help us understand this better, we could consider our ten-dimensional, timeless alien again. We need to understand how others feel, but because we cannot step outside our point of view, we need to understand this on *our* terms in order for it to make sense.

The alien lands on earth and is met by the human delegation. We see the alien responding to stimulae and, at first sight, imagine that they think in a similar way to how we do. But if they experience the world in space but not in time, then actually it must be the case that we can't imagine how they must think. If they have a mind or a consciousness, then it is something very, well – alien – not something that we can really recognise as such. However, because *we* experience the world in time, we see them move and react and we try to get a handle on their behaviour – we try to predict what they might do next. And so we may conclude that they do appear to have minds – that is to say that they behave in a way that is consistent with the behaviour of a creature with a mind.

As a next step, the delegation attempts to develop a common language for communication. The humans attempt to teach the alien the meaning of the word 'blue' through its use. It is not clear initially whether this will be possible – I remember singularly failing to teach my two year-old son how to use the word blue. But it turns out that after some familiarity with how this word is used, the aliens are able to use it correctly themselves. The humans don't know how the alien experiences 'blue' but that's fine – the humans don't know how other humans experience blue either. This is not important for communication – what matters is that the words are used correctly. The humans then teach the alien how to use the words 'before' and 'after'. It seems odd that a creature with no concept of time can use these words, but again the alien learns how to use it based on its own experience of how it is used. The alien then learns how to use the word 'time' and so even though the way it experiences the world remains a mystery to us, it is no longer accurate to say they have no concept of time. Likewise, being able to get inside the alien's head doesn't get us any further forward in understanding how its mind works, but we can still see that it does have a mind, as we would understand the concept. The alien and the humans can make no progress in getting an appreciation of each other's private experiences, but this is not a problem – each manages to understand the other on its own terms. As Wittgenstein notes in his *Philosophical Investigations* "What is hidden is of no interest to us".

One might wonder why we are so interested in what the world looks like from someone else's point of view. Does it matter if they experience the colour blue slightly differently from the way you do? It could be said that in addition to having a point of view on the world, the defining characteristics of a fully conscious being are that it has thoughts and feelings of its own. What are the implications of this?

Feelings and Other Qualia

If a being is able to feel, perhaps the key issue for us is that we want to be able to empathise with how they *really* feel and don't want to be duped. If we are consoling someone in floods of tears because their brother has died or perhaps they bashed their knee and it is streaming with blood, we would feel pretty cheated if it turned out that they weren't really feeling any pain or sorrow.

It is worth drawing a distinction here between how we *do* feel and how we *should* feel. There is more than one science fiction film which tugs at our heartstrings when the highly sophisticated robot looks at the hero with pleading eyes as it is destroyed beyond repair. Perhaps we have evolved to empathise with signs of distress irrespective of whether our intellect tells us that any real hurt has been caused. On the other hand, if we want to decide whether we *should* sympathise, we need to remember that we cannot go from an 'is' to an 'ought' and so stop to consider our values!

If our primary interest is selfish, we need to consider whether helping the robot is advantageous to us personally. Alternatively, we may consider whether it is good for society. We could consider other values, such as whether it is significant if the robot has the potential to grow or reproduce in the future. But perhaps ultimately, we want to know if the robot really is in pain, or is just simulating it. Now on the one hand, it can be argued that it should normally be very clear if the robot is in pain. Given that the meaning of the word is its use, we learn that the term being in pain applies for example, when there is tissue damage and we are crying and debilitated in some way. And perhaps this is enough. We can see that the robot typically takes actions to avoid being damaged and debilitated, and perhaps this is enough to earn it our sympathy. But perhaps what we really want to know is, is it feeling that same unpleasant sensation that *I* feel, when I am in pain? But given what we know about the ten-dimensional alien, is this really the right criterion to be judging whether sympathy is deserved? If you are unable to get a handle on what it is like to be this other being, how are you going to understand what sensations deserve sympathy?

Health professionals define pain tolerance as the maximum amount of pain that you can handle. A common test of pain tolerance is the cold pressor method. You submerge your hand into a bucket of ice-cold water, and the longer you can stand to keep your hand in the water, the higher your pain tolerance. Yet this immediately raises the question as to whether people who leave their hand in for longer are actually experiencing more pain. Could it instead be that the same environment or the same brain state causes different people different amounts of pain? Supposing someone finally withdrew their hand because the pain had reached Level 10. And suppose by some magic, you were able to experience their pain, and to your surprise you only rated it at Level 4. It is not clear that this idea makes any sense. If you rated it a four, then you are saying that the pain is bearable. But they are saying the pain reached unbearable levels. So in what sense are you experiencing *their* pain? If one person has a bearable pain and another person has an unbearable pain, then they can't be the same pain, because pain is a measure of how much it hurts. It obviously isn't hurting the person who can bear it as much as the person who can't, because if it was, they wouldn't be able to bear it either. It is measured and understood in terms of how it causes you to react.

Some may contest this and say that if you are keeping your hand in the bucket for longer, then this shows that you are taking more punishment and so experiencing more pain. Let's see if this stands up to scrutiny. Why might one person be able to hold their hand in for longer than another? Well one answer might be that the situation is not triggering the body's pain receptors to the same degree. We should be able conclude quickly here that the reason one person can keep their hand in for longer is not because they are tolerating more pain, but simply because it takes longer for them to reach the same situation in terms of pain receptor response. But let's consider the more interesting situation where the level of response provided by your pain receptors is the same for everyone. This is something that can be measured objectively (at least in principle). Would we not say that those who are coping with a higher pain receptor response before removing their hand are tolerating more pain? We would not. When we talk about pain, we are talking about a feeling, not a physical body state. Studies have shown that there is more to reported levels of pain (how much it hurts) than the degree of physical stimulus[xlviii]. I'm sure we can all think of a time when we were better able to cope with a painful situation by preparing ourselves mentally, whether this was having our teeth pulled or ripping off a plaster. This preparedness meant that it did not hurt as much as it otherwise would have and therefore that the level of pain was lower.

If the sensation experienced by another person was different to the sensation as you understand it in any *meaningful* way, for example if they feel pain differently to you or if they see the colour blue differently to you, then it would have different consequences. And so we may as well just use Occam's razor and say that they experience pain and see blue in the same way that we do. It's all a model anyway and it doesn't add any value to increase the complexity of the model with the idea that their experience involves something mysterious or different.

Let's get back to the bucket of ice-cold water. Does the person who removed their hand after only a short time deserve less sympathy, despite the fact that for them the agony was so great that they could stand it no longer? Surely someone will deserve our sympathy once they find an experience distressing enough, and this is indicated by their reaction. Our models tell us that when an entity is writhing around debilitated with severe damage, that means it is hurt. That is how we understand and make sense of that behaviour. What if the entity was only play acting? We might have come to the wrong conclusion about whether they are hurt, but if we do, it is not because we have failed to get to grips with the entity's true inner sensations. True inner sensations are a realist chimera. Rather, error here is in the empirical terms discussed in the previous chapter, regarding whether our conclusion is consistent with everything else we know about the world through our model. The error is the acknowledgement that had we modelled the entity as being in a different level of pain, this would have resulted in better explanations, like recognising the object as a bird explained why it flapped its wings.

What if the entity is a robot that doesn't have the capacity to express its pain in a way that we understand? Again, this question is confused. Under our model, being in pain is a property that an object has that allows us to make sense of certain behaviours. If these behaviours are not present then it makes no sense to consider them as being in pain[36].

Asking whether a machine is conscious is therefore analogous to asking whether someone is in pain. To answer this question, we need to flesh out our model. For me to assess if they are in pain, I need to take all the information available to me and consider whether this fits the criteria for being in pain. After I go in for a particularly heavy tackle on the football pitch, my opponent might say to me "No, it's fine. It doesn't hurt". But if I see them limping for the next five minutes, I might suspect they were not being entirely truthful. Alternatively, we might see a player rolling on the floor in agony etc. and conclude that they are in pain. But if, once the referee has given the free kick, the player gets to his feet and continues as normal, we might conclude that we were wrong and that they were only play-acting. If only we could gain direct sight of their inner feelings! Well we have already dismissed that as a blind alley. Similar considerations apply in assessing people for consciousness. If they've been knocked out and are just coming around, we might assess their level of consciousness by asking questions and judging the coherence of the responses, or perhaps in an extreme scenario by assessing their reaction to a pain stimulus. Likewise, when assessing a machine for consciousness, we probe and investigate whether it fits the criteria of consciousness. This is

[36] And if you want to ask what if they are actually in pain, despite you not considering them to be so, I can just refer you to the paragraph above.

what it *means* to be conscious – we have shown that this alternative conception of consciousness as some inaccessible aspect of an entity's true nature is incoherent. We understand consciousness on our own terms.

How do we know if a machine is only *simulating* consciousness, rather than being actually conscious? How do we know if it really feels the way it says it feels? In the same way that we know if someone is only simulating pain rather than actually being in pain. In Anything Goes metaphysics, what is *really* the case is what makes the best model. We can look carefully to try and identify signs that the pain/consciousness is not genuine. Then we make a judgement. There is no 'inner sensation'; to which we can refer. Whether machines can be conscious is a fascinating and difficult question, but the way to answer it is to consider what we mean by the term and then look to see if the machine displays those characteristics, not by trying to 'get inside its head'. A similar approach is needed when considering which animals might be said to be conscious. Are ants conscious? Scientists tell us that they although they work together to form incredibly complex structures, this does not involve wide coordination or a central plan. Rather, each ant (mindlessly?) follows a few simple rules and there is no indication that high level of consciousness is involved[xlix].

We appear to have gone full circle. We started off by saying science can't help us answer questions such as this but ended up relying on science for an answer. However, this time around we are much clearer about what the limits of science are. Anything Goes methodology is not a magic bullet that provides answers to questions such as whether God exists, or robots can be conscious. But it does help us clear up a number of confusions so that we can ask the right substantive questions. And of course, as we have seen, science is not magic either – it is just about looking closely and thinking carefully about what we see.

Thoughts and Free Will

We said that the second significant implication of a being being fully conscious, was that it has thoughts of its own. This might be a concern because it implies that such a being has its own *agency*. It is unpredictable and the actions that it takes lie outside our control. This is the consequence explored in films like Terminator and The Matrix – machines become conscious and take the decision to fight against humanity. The idea is that machines and robots start out as relatively simple constructions, which are programmable and obey the laws of nature. Then at some point, when they become sufficiently complex, they attain consciousness. An aura emerges, like a ghost rising up from the machine. It seizes control of operations and the nightmare scenario unfolds. However, this simplistic picture begins to sound a bit dubious when subjected to a modicum of scrutiny.

Firstly, as we noted above, if this 'ghost in the machine' is non-physical, we are left with that same problem of how it is supposed to interact with its physical body. Secondly and perhaps more importantly, what reason is there to believe that conscious beings are not constrained by the laws of nature? It is not clear why complex conscious beings should be any less predictable than complex unconscious systems, like the weather. This leads directly to the question of whether there is such a thing as 'free will'.

It dawns on many of us when we are learning physics at school that if the behaviour of the universe is governed by the laws of nature, then this has implications for free will. The signals received by your brain cause certain other neurons to fire which result in you taking certain actions. These are all governed by the laws of physics; the idea that *you* have the ability to influence the outcome in a way that is contrary to what would have happened if things had turned out under the laws of physics makes no sense, unless you are willing to accept the view that consciousness is somehow exempt from the laws of nature. Or to put it less controversially, we could say that if we accept that free will exists, then our understanding of the laws of nature is incomplete, because they cannot accommodate free will in their current form.

However, if you believe in causation – that the universe is deterministic, then this does seem to rule out the concept of free will. And so the idea that your actions were the result of a free choice made by you is just an illusion. This idea was more formally put by American philosopher Peter Van Inwagen in 1983, as follows

"If determinism is true, then our acts are the consequences of the laws of nature and events in the remote past. But it is not up to us what went on before we were born, and neither is it up to us what the laws of nature are. Therefore, the consequences of these things (including our present acts) are not up to us."

Perhaps quantum theory can help us out here. We might hope that if events in the universe are spontaneous, rather than caused, this might provide room for free will to make a comeback. However it is difficult to see how a decision that just happens randomly, due to a quantum event in your brain, for example, could be reasonably attributed to resulting from your personal choice.

Of course, while many of us recognise the difficulties with free will at an intellectual level, we tend to disregard them in everyday life. After all, it certainly seems to *us* that our choices are free. But let's stop and consider for a minute what it means to say that our choices are free. In a weak sense, we might think that a free choice is a choice we make with no overt pressure to choose one option over another. This contrasts with a choice made at gunpoint, for example. But then again, would we say that a nicotine addict freely chooses to smoke? In a stronger sense, we might say that free will involves the ability to make a choice at all. It is where an action involves you making a decision, rather than it just being a reflex action, like the knee-jerk reaction or a jump scare. It is interesting to consider the proportion of the actions that we take which could be said to be the result of a conscious decision. You might make a decision to walk down the street in order to go to the local shop. But as you are walking, you are not thinking "I'll put my left foot here, and then after that I'll put my right foot there" and so on; it all 'just happens' automatically while you are thinking about other things. If we do stop to think about these actions, we are very good at finding reasons for them. "I hit the brake pedal because I was approaching a sharp bend". "I yelled at them because they were being unreasonable". "I chose tea, because that was what I was in the mood for". What does happen when someone offers us a choice between tea or coffee? We find ourselves thinking "I quite fancy a cup of tea, please". Or more likely, we find ourselves *saying* "a cup of tea, please". It is quite rare that we rehearse what we are going to say before actually saying it. But even conscious decisions might be said to be things that 'just happen'. It is very rare that we decide in advance to make a decision. Perhaps an example of this might be those occasions when there is some decision that we are putting off. But to avoid an infinite regress, the first decision will have to 'just happen'. Imagine you are about to go to the shops when you realise that it is raining heavily. Do you decide to go now or wait? Isn't the most accurate way of characterising what happens to say that you observe the decision taken by your brain? If you are not convinced, try the following thought experiment. Firstly, consider the following two meals and make a decision as to which you would rather have for dinner later: Option 1 – Salted Cod Souffle, Mallaig Scallops, Sea Bass and Crispy Capers in a Lemon Butter Sauce or Option 2 – 8oz Ribeye Steak, Herb Roasted Tomatoes, Battered Onion Rings, Hand Cut Chips and Peppercorn Sauce. Now for the second part, let's imagine that you are a skilled mage and that by some wizardry, you are able spiritwalk and piggyback onto the mind of someone else. You are a silent observer, able to see what they see, feel what they feel, and experience their thoughts real time, and they have no idea you are there. You attain a Zen level of quiet and have no thoughts of your own during this exercise. This person is asked to make a choice between the following desserts: Coconut & Passionfruit Cheesecake or Vanilla Panna Cotta, Mixed Berry Compote & Mini Meringues. You note them picturing the different components of the dishes and imagining the smells and tastes. You share their feeling of attraction towards one of these options, and you note that it also occurs to them that one dish might be healthier. A few seconds later, you note them thinking "Erm, yes, I'll go for that one". Now my question for you is this – can it really be said that there is *more* going on in the first scenario where you are making the decision, than in the second scenario where you are just observing a decision being made by someone else? I suggest that 'making a decision' just amounts to first hand observation of a decision being made; there is no evidence that you have any more control over the decision that emerges in the first scenario than you have in the second. I would challenge anyone who claims otherwise, to explain how this comes about. You cannot decide in advance what you are going to think – your thoughts are just those that occur to you at the time[37].

And it is worth noting that reasons are not always the same as causes. I might reason that I did a chicken impression because I was in a particularly irreverent mood. The cause may be that I had been hypnotised. But what we don't find is that we had taken a decision to do one thing and then found to our surprise that our body did something else! That somehow we were not in control of our own bodies. This 'compatibilist' conception of free will argues that we do have free will in the sense that we have the agency to be able to do as we want[l].

What would be the implications for society if the concept of free will was rejected and it was instead accepted that no-one has any ability to influence the actions that they take? Does this give people a licence to no longer put effort into making the 'right' choices? I may as well just do what I want, given that I have no control over the outcome and what will be will be. However the broader factors that governed our choices previously haven't gone away. People will still stop smoking if they want to live a long time and stop using fossil fuels if they want life on our planet to thrive. So perhaps the primary impact would be psychological – we have a new excuse to justify taking an unpopular decision. Morally, the main impact is in terms of accountability or blame. Is it reasonable to punish people for actions deemed morally wrong, if they have no control over them? Punishments may still have their use as deterrents or re-education tools, but is it fair to hold people responsible for actions over which they have no control?

Arguably society is already moving in this direction. We are perhaps less prone than in times past to categorise people as inherently 'good' or 'bad' and look instead for the reasons behind certain actions. We may ascribe

---

[37] It might be argued that you can train yourself to think certain thoughts. For example, after losing many games of chess, I now routinely think about whether any of my pieces are under attack before making the next move. Did I freely choose to keep practicing chess? And despite all the practice, sometimes I will forget and exclaim 'Oh no my queen!' . However much we try to set ourselves up for success, we can't know in advance what our next thought will be.

antisocial behaviour to factors in the person's upbringing and criminals may claim diminished responsibility. We are confident that certain environmental factors will lead people 'down the wrong track'. And we can predict what the consequences will be – the fact that people are conscious and have minds of their own does not necessarily make them unpredictable. Aunty Joan may think she is using her free will when she decides to travel by train, but I could predict that she would choose this, given how scared she is of flying. So it is not obvious that an AI attaining consciousness means it is suddenly less predictable and less under our control.

So to sum up, to understand whether a future sophisticated AI is conscious and has a point of view on the world, we start by looking at whether its behaviours are in line with what we would expect from a conscious being. This is something we can be right or wrong about in the everyday sense. If there was no reason to view the AI as having any thoughts or feelings of its own, then it would be incorrect to view it as conscious – we know the kind of thing we are talking about when we talk about conscious beings, and this AI is clearly not one of them. However, with more advanced AIs, answering this question becomes more challenging. When people engage in dialogues with the latest AI, large language models such as ChatGPT can give a very good impression of thinking for themselves[li]. Now if we were to come across an AI that behaves as though fully conscious, I hope I have shown above that whether the AI is actually conscious, rather than just simulating it, is a metaphysical choice. Just like the question of whether other people have minds of their own, or whether God exists, it is not a fact about the world that we can be right or wrong about. But as in the case when trying to understand other people, our best way of making sense of AI is look at it long and hard and see what way of thinking about it best fits in with the rest of our model.

In 2023, we are still some way off seeing robots that meet the definition of being fully conscious, but it is important for many of us to take these questions seriously and look into them deeply, because of the moral implications. Compare the way we treat our pets, who we view as conscious, with the way we might step on a bug without any qualms, secure in the belief that it is not conscious and so no harm has been done. Might it be the case that in several generations' time, society views insects as conscious creatures and so deplores the way society treats them today? We would want to know if it is appropriate to view a particular AI as a conscious being in order to be able to treat it in line with our values.

So deciding whether AIs are conscious comes back to carefully inspecting the information provided by our own experiences and choosing a suitable model. Sadly Anything Goes methodology does not provide any shortcuts or means to avoid doing the hard yards of looking and thinking and coming to a view. As with everything else we have discussed, the more effort you are prepared to put in to forming a coherent map of your experiences that works for you, the more harmonious your reality and the smoother life's journey will be.

Schrödinger's Cat revisited

What other problems can be solved with this new way of understanding consciousness? Physicists such as E.P Wigner have claimed that the unique characteristics of human consciousness may contain the key to unlocking the conundrum of Schrödinger's Cat introduced in chapter 6. Recall that one of the first indications we had that there was something wrong with the common-sense picture of the universe was with the development of quantum physics and the discovery of the measurement problem. As a reminder, the quantum state of a system is not determined until it is measured. It is not just that the state is *unknown* until it is measured, but that it actually *has no* definitive state until it is measured. This might remind us of Kant's Ontological Denial which says that the Superunknowable has no meaningful structure outside of the way we experience it. These quantum ideas led to the thought experiment of Schrödinger's Cat. A quantum system, such as a photon going through a polariser, a lethal device and a cat are put in a sealed box. If the photon emerges through the left-hand channel of the polariser, the lethal device is triggered and the cat is killed. If the photon emerges through the right-hand channel, the device is not triggered and the cat survives. Because the channel through which the photon passed is only actualised when the box is opened, until that point, the cat is neither alive nor dead, which is ridiculous.

There is an alternative version of the thought experiment known as 'Wigner's Friend'. Instead of a cat in the box, we have Wigner's Friend, often referred to as Alice. And to persuade Alice to take part in the thought experiment, we replace the lethal device with a detector which records the channel of the polariser through which the photon passes. We open the box at 12:00 and find that the photon passed through the left hand channel. Because this is a quantum system, it was only at the point of opening the box, at 12:00 that the photon could be said to have any kind of polarisation. Before that, it was suspended in a quantum superposition of states, awaiting measurement and Wigner's friend could not be said to have observed it in either state. However, when we speak to Wigner's friend, she informs us that she observed the detector registering the photon as having passed through the left-hand channel at 11:37. What are we to make of this? The earliest time that we know of the photon being in a definite state is 11:37, when Wigner's friend made the observation. This is when a human mind first made the measurement and provides us with the certainty we need to be able to say that a measurement has been made. This raises the question of what it is about the human mind, that causes particular changes in the world around us, namely that causes a world of potential states to crystalise into a world of actual states – in this case that causes a photon to pass through one or other channel of a polariser.

Where are we going with this? If the human consciousness can somehow effect changes in physical systems, this seems incredible, and our scientific theories don't even begin to suggest how this might be done. And what is it that is unique about consciousness that can effect these changes? Does this provide a scientific basis for believing in the 'soul' for example – some part of our nature that is non-physical? If this explanation doesn't sound credible then there are others. One of the most popular interpretations is the 'many worlds' hypothesis, first suggested by Hugh Everett III in 1957[lii]. Under the many worlds hypothesis, each time a quantum event takes place, the universe splits into two (or more). In the case above, we have one universe where the photon passed through the left hand channel and a parallel universe where it passed through the right-hand channel. Wigner's friend tells you at 12:00 that she observed the photon having passed through the left hand channel, but in a parallel universe there is a copy of Wigner's friend telling a copy of you that she observed it going through the right hand channel. Given that quantum events are taking place all around us, all the time, this leads to the idea that there are possibly an infinite number of universes out there existing in parallel to our own! Surely there must be a way of interpreting the results of quantum mechanics, that is not quite so outlandish?

*

The realist, common-sense picture has a clear demarcation between the world as we experience it, and the world as it is in itself. This is difficult to reconcile with the results of quantum mechanics, which say that the way things are depend on whether they have been observed. I might think that there is a guitar hanging on the wall behind me, but Quantum Mechanics says there is no wall behind me until I turn my head and observe it. Until that point, there is just a superposition of states and a high probability that when I turn around, it will resolve itself into a wall. That's all very well for objects such as a wall. But how do we fit objects such as other people into this scheme? Are they observers, or quantum objects being observed or both?

With our new understanding however, the thought experiment presents no conceptual problems and there is no need to venture into the realm of the fantastic to try to make sense of it. Instead of saying that the world is a quantum superposition of states, awaiting a human consciousness to trigger collapse into a particular state, we take the first person perspective. My (your) 'world' can be treated as a quantum superposition of states and it is my (your) observations only that trigger collapse. As discussed above when considering consciousness, Anything Goes methodology turns the order of explanation on its head, and starts with our experiences. Yes, the universe behaves as if the cat is neither alive nor dead for me until I observe it. I can be comfortable with this using Anything Goes methodology, because there are no such things as disembodied facts about whether the cat is alive or dead. There are only facts for me. But what are the facts for the cat, one may ask? We are now back in familiar territory. Let's return to Wigner's friend.

Wigner's friend makes her measurement of the photon's polarisation and then slips a note under the door of the lab, letting Wigner know that she has made the measurement, and the photon has been detected in one particular state. But as she hasn't told Wigner *which* state the photon has been detected in, as far as Wigner is concerned, no measurement has been made and the quantum system is still in a superposition of both states. So what is the 'true' situation? Experiments have been conducted to simulate a version of the Wigner's Friend thought experiment and the results are in line with the theoretical predictions[liii]. We are left with the conclusion that either it is reasonable to state that a 'fact about the world' might be true for one person but at the same time false for someone else, or quantum mechanics is wrong (or at least, is not universally applicable). The idea that the claims of quantum theory are observer dependent is championed by interpretations such as relational quantum mechanics or QBism[liv], which have much in common with Anything Goes thinking. The quantum model is a model of *my* universe, rather than facts about *the* universe. Quantum mechanics is better thought of as a model of our experiences as individuals; of how the universe behaves for me (or from your perspective, for you). When looking at things at a higher level, I can be happy that for Wigner's friend, it is a model of how it behaves for him. But strictly, quantum mechanics says that neither the wall, the cat nor Wigner's friend exist until we observe them. It might sound crazy to argue that Wigner's friend doesn't exist unless I am talking to her – how does that work from her point of view? She obviously doesn't feel herself popping in and out of existence depending on whether or not I am looking at her! But of course, the same thing applies to my own body!

The Schrödinger's Cat thought experiment looks to highlight the problem of finding the boundary between the quantum and the everyday world. If it is accepted, as many physicists do, that quantum mechanics applies to whole world, rather than just the sub-atomic world, then the question is not whether the cat is alive or dead while inside the box, but Berkeley's more basic question about whether the cat can be considered to exist at all when unperceived (unmeasured). "But which model should I be using?!" I hear you howl! If quantum mechanics is the map and the map is the territory, then either I have to accept that Wigner's friend really doesn't exist unperceived or I cannot accept quantum mechanics, even though that best explains the data.

Realists just can't cope with these implications, which are incompatible with their underlying beliefs. They start twitching and something goes 'ping' inside their rigid inflexible minds. But, being familiar with Anything Goes methodology we can be relaxed about this. I know that the universe as it is in itself is unknowable, and the entities in it only exist as objects for me. As we noted above, when an entity only exists in the first place as an object-for-me, it doesn't make sense to talk about whether it has a consciousness outside of how we perceive it. So we don't have to worry about the consciousness' continuity through time in the capacity of a thing-in-itself. Realists start panicking if you suggest that it might not be the case that there is a single 'way the world *is*', if only we could find it. Anything Goes adherents on the other hand, acknowledge that we use different models for different purposes. Given that the probability of the wall and Wigner's friend existing as expected when I turn to observe them is effectively certain, it is reasonable for day-to-day purposes, to see them (model them) as entities that exist in their own right. The map is the territory. It is only by treating the quantum model in a realist sense that you get into difficulties – because under a realist position it makes no sense for a system to have properties for one person but not for another.

It is instructive to consider the parallel with the way the light inside a refrigerator is triggered by opening the door. One might think that the light inside the fridge is always on, because whenever you open the door, you can see that this is the case. Or imagine you are in a dark room with a torch that only shines green light. You might think that all the objects in the room are green, because whenever you focus on them, so they are. When you are not focusing on them, you may as well continue to consider them as green if you have no idea as to how else they could be configured.

In the same way, although quantum mechanics tells me that the wall behind me doesn't exist until I experience it or Wigner's friend doesn't exist until I interact with her, it is more useful for me to consider them as continuing to exist during this time, because when I next interact with them, it will be as if they always did. An object near my blind spot may be blurry, but my model tells me that when I focus on it, it will be sharp. These ideas give scientific realists headaches, because they want to know what the 'real' situation is at any given time. Practitioners of Anything Goes metaphysics on the other hand, are relaxed, understanding that it's all models.

The Schrödinger's Cat thought experiment brings to light some of the problems that arise when quantum mechanics is thought of as a description of the reality in which we all live. In particular, it conflicts with the idea that other people, or cats, are a different kind of thing to the objects, the behaviour of which is being described. This is because the concept of measurement is at the fore and so paradoxes arise if there are many people doing the measuring. If, on the other hand, quantum mechanics is thought of as a description of the behaviour of objects of our experience, then other people have no special status. You are the only one doing any measuring and the paradox is resolved.

Chapter 15

15. Into the Future

Over the course of our investigations, there has been a lot of heavy lifting, and I have argued that we have been able to complete our understanding of whether God exists. As well as answering this question, I suggest that along the way we have also gained a deeper understanding of what it means for something to exist and how to view the nature of the world around us. I have argued that the scientific realist, common sense approach overreaches itself in terms of its claims about what can be known and is dogmatic in its statements about the way things are – it is just one of a number of possible ways of making sense of our experiences and while this works well at the everyday level, it leads to confusion when it comes to the question of whether God exists. I have tried to show that Anything Goes methodology allows us to answer the question of whether God exists in a satisfactory manner, while still preserving common sense at the everyday level.

In particular, we saw that the existence of a reality that persists independently of us is an assumption, and that even if true, knowledge of the nature of this independent reality is forever beyond our reach. We saw that everything we speak of or think about that is meaningful to us relates to our perspective on reality; our map or model of the ways our experiences behave. This led us to re-evaluate what we mean by 'existence' and resulted in a world that is for each of us intensely *personal.* We saw that The Map *is* the Territory, when everything that is meaningful forms part of the Map. It may be the case that you have a God and I don't and vice versa. It is up to each of us to find a way of making sense of our world that we find satisfying, whether this be through an established religion or no religion at all. You may even find your own way that works just for you! Finally, we saw that it is other people that keep us grounded by securing the meaning of the words we use and stop us from spiralling off into a world where the Truth is whatever you want it to be.

From this perspective, I would go as far as to say that the question of whether God exists is settled. A true theistic believer understands their experiences as a result of the interventions of God and we have no grounds to dispute this. But it is important to stress that a metaphysical explanation is different to a scientific explanation, in that a scientific explanation is subject to experimental verification. The Anything Goes approach essentially extends the scope of the scientific method to untestable areas, but since they are untestable, the choice of which metaphysical model to apply to your experiences is a matter of personal preference – of which model seems right to you. But because the metaphysical model cannot be falsified, we have to respect others' choices in this regard if we respect them as human beings. "You'd better pray to your Gods", says the native to the captured intruder, capturing the Anything Goes spirit in the process. An atheist on the other hand, understands their experiences as a result of physical processes that have no deific aspect. And we likewise need to respect this if we respect them as human beings. What about followers of different religions who believe in different Gods? If you accept that there are other people in this world with their own points of view that we interact with, then they will have their own way of experiencing the world. Their Gods are as real for them as yours are for you. Therefore the only way of claiming that their Gods are less legitimate is if you don't accept other people as equals, with an equal right to their own perspective on our common reality.

Of course, there will be those who feel strongly that a world with God is a better place to be, and such evangelists may want to do all they can to help others see the world in this way. Under the Anything Goes approach, such a position would view the atheist stance as sad but legitimate. This is different to societies or hardliners that view unbelievers as infidels, and reject their views as illegitimate.

Yet what about the agnostic perspective? Those who are certain that God either does or does not exist have no need to read a book that explores this question, and so it is likely that most readers are those who were uncertain as to whether God exists under the common-sense approach. How have things changed now that we understand that the Map is the Territory? Is there still room for sitting on the fence?

When the Map is the Territory, we are considering whether God exists in a de facto sense. So what kind of agnostic are we considering? Is it a believer with occasional moments of doubt? In this case, God is a feature of their lives. They pray to God to help their loved ones and for guidance in times of fear and indecision. For this person, God clearly exists as a living, breathing part of their lives. The Anything Goes approach shows that it is wrongheaded to question whether God 'really exists'; if it appears to be the case that God is there, providing guidance and support, then so he is. If on the other hand, we are considering a less spiritual soul, who normally proceeds through life without giving the existence of God a second thought, then God does not exist in a de facto sense and hence does not exist at all. This person, when benighted by the common-sense picture, may have wondered whether there is a chance that they got it wrong and that God may exist. We have now seen that this worry is completely groundless; they can continue their heathen atheistic ways with confidence! Now there are those who behave as pragmatic atheists the majority of the time, but in times of acute stress and turmoil, may turn to God and pray for a miracle. This highlights the difference between hope and belief. As stated previously, our choice of metaphysics provides a framework in which to understand our experiences, but it doesn't give us knowledge of the future. We all might hope for a miracle in times of desperation; these prayers are made more in desperation than in any expectation that they will have an effect.

*

The job of this book is not to say that any particular way of looking at things is wrong or right. The point of the Anything Goes approach is to understand that it is up to you how you make sense of your own experiences. Other people can try to help you live more harmoniously by pointing out alternative ways of looking at things, but ultimately it is your life and your experiences and up to you how you make sense of them. We made the point above that the world that each of us live in is intensely *personal.* Next time you look at the trees swaying in the wind, the sunlight shining through the clouds or simply observe the world passing by, why not reflect on the fact that this is *your* world? This isn't the world as it is in itself, which has no intelligible form or structure. It is the world as lived in by *you.* Close your eyes for a minute and listen to those sounds; smell those smells. To be alive in the Superunknowable means that this huge, vastly complex world around you is yours alone! Other people may have their versions of it, but only you get to experience it like this. What a treat! Aren't we lucky to be born with a make-up that allows us to experience a world with such beauty and depth?

*

One of the aims mentioned right at the beginning of the book was to provide a firmer footing on which we can move forward as a society, so it is worth considering whether the Anything Goes approach achieves this. Certainly, one might hope that with an understanding of the subjective nature of the structure of reality, might come more acceptance of differing views. But we also saw that the Anything Goes approach demands a certain maturity; it demands that people can be honest with themselves. In the face of disagreement or when faced with unpleasant truths, it is perhaps all too easy to fall back on the fact that the Map is the Territory and insist that anything you want to be true is in fact true for you. The price of this bloody-mindedness is that such people continue to face a life of struggle, with experiences in conflict with their beliefs as they continue to try to force square pegs into round holes. Those, on the other hand, who can adapt their perspective to fit their experiences, are rewarded with a life of harmony.

End Notes

Chapter 1

[i] For a thoughtful account of how societies have evolved in tandem with their deities, see, for example, the article by Philip Bell in Nature (4 March 2015) titled "Complex societies evolved without belief in all-powerful deity". Essentially anthropological in character, the article looks at analysis which investigated the relationship between the complexity of a society and its form of religion. Bell notes that all human societies have been shaped by religion and looks in particular at belief in a "big God" (an all-powerful, punitive deity who sits in moral judgement on our actions) as well as other forms of religion, such as polytheism and a belief in the power of karma or ancestral spirits. He argues that belief in a Big God co-evolved with social and political complexity and goes on to discuss which drives which.

[ii] For more on the degree to which atheism captured the popular imagination in ancient times, see Tim Whitmarsh's book 'Battling the Gods - Atheism in the ancient world '(New York: Alfred A. Knopf, 2015). In this unusual book, Whitmarsh explores the role of religion in ancient Greece and Rome. Whitmarsh argues that priests were functionaries rather than sources of moral or cosmological wisdom and that the absence of centralised religious authority allowed for an exceptional diversity of perspectives on sacred matters, ranging from devotional practises to organised religion right through to the atheos, of the "godless."

[iii] For a number of detailed examples on the direct experience of God, see William P. Alston's 'Perceiving God' (Cornell University Press, 1991). Alston argues that incidents of perceiving God directly contribute significantly to the basis of religious belief and goes on to make the case for how this can be justified.

[iv] Christianity: A Very Short Introduction (Linda Woodhead, 2014) has a good section from Chapter 6 onwards, covering how Christianity in its various forms has adapted to a changing world.

Chapter 2

[v] There are plenty of places to go to find more information on the traditional arguments for the existence of God; and in particular the Design Argument, the Cosmological Argument and the Ontological Argument. The Internet Encyclopaedia of Philosophy ('IEP') has a section on the first of these here: https://iep.utm.edu/design-arguments-for-existence-of-god/ and also briefly covers the Cosmological and Ontological arguments on it's the Philosophy of Religion page.

The Stanford Encyclopaedia of Philosophy covers the Cosmological and Ontological arguments in more detail online at https://plato.stanford.edu/entries/cosmological-argument/ and https://plato.stanford.edu/entries/ontological-arguments/. Their discussion on the Ontological Argument is however very technical. For a reasonably comprehensive and readable discussion of these traditional arguments, I would recommend T, J. Mawson's book 'Belief in God' (Oxford University Press, 2005)

[vi] David Hume is towering figure in western philosophy and just one of the things he is celebrated for is his insistence that we have no justification for believing that certain events cause other events. This is because all we see are a series of correlations – it is now seen as sage advice when investigating some phenomenon or other to remember that 'correlation does not necessarily imply a causal connection'. This is a point that I explore in more detail later in the book, especially in chapters 7 and 8.

[vii] A very readable introduction to these modern arguments for the existence of God can be found in Peter Vardy's 'The Puzzle of God' (Routledge, 1997).

[viii] What do we mean when we say a statement is true? What can we infer if we are told that a statement is true? For a comprehensive, if technical, discussion on different theories of truth, see the Stanford Encyclopaedia of Philosophy entry at https://plato.stanford.edu/entries/truth/

[ix] Verificationism is a theory that emerged in the early 20th century that tried to clear away a lot of the uncertainty commonly found in linguistic statements. Verificationism asserts that unless a statement could be verified as either true or false, then it should be rejected as nonsense. Although popular for a time, it fell out of fashion when it became clear firstly that there are a lot of statements that we all treat as perfectly meaningful, which are unverifiable and secondly it was not clear how strict the requirement of verifiability is. If a newspaper provides evidence of a past event, is this verified or could the newspaper be wrong? A final challenge was that Verificationism might be thought of as nonsense based on its own definition! Can it be verified that only meaningful statements are verifiable ones? The Stanford Encyclopaedia of Philosophy has more on verificationism on its Logical Positivism page https://plato.stanford.edu/entries/logical-empiricism/

[x] For more on Fictionalism, see 'A Critical Introduction to Fictionalism' by Frederick Kroon, Jonathan McKeown-Green and Stuart Brock (Bloomsbury, 2018).

[xi] 'Faith after Foundationalism' by Welsh philosopher of religion D. Z. Phillips (Routledge, 1988) is a readable critique that goes through several modern ways of interpreting religious faith, championing an anti-realist position.

Chapter 3

[xii] A comprehensive resource on Newton's life and works is online at https://www.newtonproject.ox.ac.uk/

[xiii] Einstein's views on religion are notoriously difficult to pin down, and both atheists and theists have quoted him in support of their views. It seems clear that he rejected the personal God that we know from Christianity, but held a wonder for the mysterious spirit or forces that drive the universe. Whether this is a personification of natural forces or something more has been a matter of debate. To learn more, you could try Max Jammer's 'Einstein and Religion' (Princeton University Press, 2002).

[xiv] The full report on this study can be downloaded from https://www.researchgate.net/publication/7208885_Study_of_the_Therapeutic_Effects_of_Intercessory_Prayer_STEP_in_Cardiac_Bypass_Patients_A_Multicenter_Randomized_Trial_of_Uncertainty_and_Certainty_of_Receiving_Intercessory_Prayer/download?_tp=eyJjb250ZXh0Ijp7ImZpcnN0UGFnZSI6InB1YmxpY2F0aW9uIiwicGFnZSI6InB1YmxpY2F0aW9uIn19

Chapter 4

xv Bishop George Berkeley is a leading figure in idealist or immaterialist thought, which says that the objects that we interact with don't have any real existence of their own. He studied at Trinity College in Dublin, became a fellow in 1707 and later travelled extensively in Europe and America. For more about Berkeley, see for example, the entry at the Internet Encyclopedia of Philosophy site https://iep.utm.edu/george-berkeley-british-empiricist/

xvi For an excellent introduction to how the brain works, you could try New Scientist's 'How Your Brain Works' (John Murray Learning, 2017), which is part of their 'Instant Expert' series. It covers recent development in neuroscience and goes over what this can tell us about features such as memory, intelligence, emotions, sleep, sensations and consciousness.

xvii For an excellent book that explores this line of thinking, try Andy Clark's 'The Experience Machine' (Allen Lane, 2023). On this view, supported by recent developments in neuroscience, the picture we have of the world is a kind of 'controlled hallucination'. Rather than merely reflecting the incoming information from our senses, the brain tries to predict what we see, based on past experiences.

xviii John Locke's 'An Essay Concerning Human Understanding' was an influential milestone of Western philosophy by one of the three great British Empiricists (the other two being Berkeley and Hume), and is available to read in full at https://www.gutenberg.org/files/10615/10615-h/10615-h.htm.

Chapter 5

xix How is it that we came to know all the things we think we now know about life, the universe and everything? The history of scientific discovery is a vast topic and it is difficult to recommend one book that covers it all. Perhaps you might start with Bill Bryon's 'A Short History of Nearly Everything' (Black Swan, 2004) as a readable introduction.

xx It is Young Earth Creationism that advocates interpreting the Bible literally, when it comes to the age of the Earth. Old Earth Creationism views the Bible as compatible with the scientific position if the Bible is interpreted allegorically. This raises the issue of how young Earth creationists respond to the claims made by science. While some look to contest scientific findings as unreliable, others fall back on the idea that God created the earth 6,000 years ago, such that it *appeared* to be much older. This tactic exploits the broader sceptical worry that generally things may not be how they appear to be. For more on the defence of Young Earth Creationism, see https://www.gotquestions.org/old-earth-vs-young-earth.html

xxi If you want to find out more about any of these fascinating facts about the way the universe works, then there are loads of videos on Youtube – some better than others. For reading more, I would recommend 'The Fabric of the Cosmos' by Brian Greene (Penguin, 2005) or 'A Universe from Nothing' by Lawrence M. Kraus (Simon and Schuster, 2012) which has a focus on what we know about how the universe began.

Chapter 6

[xxii] For an explanation of how forces can be seen in terms of particle exchange, see this Arvin Ash YouTube video: https://www.youtube.com/watch?v=gkHmXhhAF2Y

[xxiii]

https://twitter.com/MaltesersUK/status/778946202163347458?s=20&t=zEBTDuNg6YSmOsPDY1pzPg.

[xxiv] This example is taken from 'Quantum Physics: Illusion or Reality' by Alastair Rae (Cambridge University Press, 1994). This short book explores the various ways that scientists and philosophers have tried to interpret the confusing results of subatomic experiments and contrasts the standard 'Copenhagen interpretation' with a number of competing ways of seeing things. Rae's book really helps us get to grips with the fundamental differences between the quantum mechanical world and the common-sense picture. Some chapters take concentration and perseverance to get the most out of them, but it provides a deeper understanding than the more superficial introductions that can be obtained from pop-science books.

Chapter 7

[xxv] The ideas of quantum physics are so counter-intuitive, that many physicists have looked to see if it may be possible to provide an alternative common sense explanation for the results of sub-atomic experiments. One such idea was put forward by Albert Einstein, Boris Podolski and Nathan Rosen in their 1935 paper titled "Can Quantum-Mechanical Description of Physical Reality be Considered Complete?", which came to be known as the 'EPR' paper This argued against the idea that the results of one experiment can be instantly affected by the results of another experiment that took place far away – this idea of action-at-a-distance should be impossible if a signal cannot travel faster than the speed of light. Instead, the EPR paper suggested that the outcome of both experiments is determined by 'hidden variables'.

In the experiments in question, the results are correlated. We might be measuring the spin of two electrons or the polarisation of two photons, but we set the experiment up such that if one experiment results in a spin 'Up' measurement, the experiment on the other electron will result in a spin 'Down' measurement. Standard quantum mechanics says that before measurement, the electrons have no spin. When one is measured, the result will be random. Let's says it results in spin 'Up'. Then by spooky action-at-a-distance, the other electron now far away is immediately guaranteed to have gone from having no spin to spin 'Down'. EPR says this is crazy. EPR says instead that before measurement, one had spin 'Up' and the other had spin 'Down', we just did not know which was which. This is known as 'local realism'. According to local realism, all particles have definite properties for all possible measurements (realism) and communication between particles is no faster than the speed of light. The electrons had spin, we just did not know which electron had which. So when one electron is measured as spin 'Up' we can know that the other must be spin 'Down' because it always had the opposite spin. It is just our knowledge that is changing – there is nothing physically changing, so there is no need for any magical action-at-a-distance. This is covered in more detail in this video: https://www.youtube.com/watch?v=Y9hBBdaZUHc

This alternative EPR explanation raised the question of how to tell which of the two explanations was correct. In 1964, the Northern Irish physicist John Stewart Bell came up with a test, known as Bell's Theorem or the Bell Inequality. There are

---

several versions of this test, but it essentially says that firstly you make a lot of measurements of spin or polarisation for correlated pairs of electrons or protons, and then combine these measurements in a certain way to get a number. Bell realised that if local realism is true, this resultant number will always be less than some value. The mathematical equation is based on the idea that if local realism is true, then the expected value of the two measurements can be expressed as the product of the expected value of the individual measurements, each conditional on the underlying correlation. If you are interested in the detail of how this is derived, an explanation of the CHSH version of the Bell inequality can be found here: https://www.youtube.com/watch?v=hZX7wUdFSOQ

The 2022 Nobel Prize in physics went to John Clauser, Alain Aspect and Anton Zeilinger for their work in recent decades showing the Bell inequality being violated in experiments and so that local realism as defined above is not true. It must be the case that either something is travelling faster than the speed of light or the particles do not have definite values until they are measured. See more on this here: https://www.youtube.com/watch?v=9OMojSTeeBg&t=18s

[xxvi] To learn more about dark matter and dark energy, see for example Brian Clegg's 'Dark Matter and Dark Energy' (Icon Books, 2019) or Lawrence M. Krauss' 'A Universe From Nothing' (Simon and Schuster, 2012)

[xxvii] For the story behind the discovery of the Higgs Boson, you could try Sean Carrol's 'The Particle at the End of the Universe' (Dutton, 2013).

[xxviii] For more on String theory, see 'The Fabric of the Cosmos' by Brian Greene (Penguin, 2005) or you could start with this short introductory video from the Swiss National Science Foundation: https://www.youtube.com/watch?v=Da-2h2B4faU.

[xxix] Don Cupitt's 'The Long-Legged Fly' (SCM Press Ltd, 1987) provides a good exploration of how these revisionist views are intended to be understood from one of their principal advocates. Don Cupitt (born 22 May 1934) is a philosopher of religion and a scholar of Christian theology and one of the best-known revisionists in the anti-realist camp.

[xxx] Popper's theory of Falsificationism is a staple component of courses on the Philosophy of Science and there is plenty of information about this available for free online. A good introduction to the philosophy of science can be found in Peter Godfrey-Smith's 'Theory and Reality' (University of Chicago Press, 2003).

[xxxi] A vigorous argument pushing the view that theories cannot be falsified was put forward by W.V.O. Quine in his famous paper 'Two Dogmas of Empiricism' which was published in 1951.

[xxxii] The original paper, 'A Confutation of Convergent Realism' (Larry Laudan, March 1981, Philosophy of Science Vol. 48, No. 1), Harding and Rosenberg's reply 'In Defense of Convergent Realism' (Clyde L. Hardin and Alexander Rosenberg, December 1982, Philosophy of Science Vol. 49, No. 4) and Laudan's response 'Realism with the Real' (Larry Laudan, March 1984, Philosophy of Science Vol. 51, No. 1) can all be found online.

Chapter 8

xxxiii Kant details his philosophy regarding the limits of human knowledge in what is widely considered to be one of the greatest achievements in Western philosophy – 'The Critique of Pure Reason' published in 1781 (second edition 1787). His work is intended to resolve the great tension in philosophy that existed at the time between the rationalism championed by those such as Leibniz and the empiricism of Locke and Hume. Kant's 'Transcendental Idealism' is positioned as a third way, that rejects the perceived errors of both. An excellent book on this subject is Sebastian Gardner's 'Kant and the Critique of Pure Reason' (Routledge 1999).

xxxiv Note that the rate at which time passes for each of us is a different question. It is perhaps a well-known fact that 'flies see in slow motion' i.e. the passage of time is slower for flies than it is for humans, which is why a fly has plenty of time to get out of the way, even when we try to swat it in an instant. However, for both a fly and a human, the earth will still take one day to rotate (by definition); the fly just perceives a day as taking longer than a human does. See the following link to an article in The Guardian that covers how this idea has been explored. Studies indicate a link between perception of time and metabolic rate, with smaller creatures appearing to experience time passing more slowly
https://www.theguardian.com/science/2013/sep/16/time-passes-slowly-flies-study

Chapter 9

xxxv The Internet Encyclopedia of Philosophy page on solipsism makes the case that the whole idea is incoherent and can be found here: https://iep.utm.edu/solipsis/. These arguments are usually explored with reference to the Problem of Other Minds and typically use Wittgensteinian ideas about what we mean by the words we use. We will explore this further in Parts II and III.

Chapter 10

xxxvi Wittgenstein produced two major philosophical works – the *Tractatus Logico-Philosophicus* published in 1922 and *Philosophical Investigations* published in 1953. The two works are several decades apart, and Wittgenstein's philosophy matured markedly over that period. The idea that the meaning of words is indicated by their use is championed in his later works. Wittgenstein does not go out of his way to make life easy for his readers and it does take some effort to get to grips with what he is saying. On the other hand, later works such as the *Philosophical Investigations* are quite readable and largely free from technical jargon, which he grew to abhor.

xxxvii I should qualify this by saying that the meaning of mu presented here is that given in modern popular literature.

Chapter 11

xxxviii Bertrand Russell wrote in 1903 "Words have meaning in the simple sense that they are symbols that stand for something other than themselves". This was part of a broader attempt to introduce more clarity over concepts and more logical rigour into philosophical argument that developed in the early part of the 20th century and was pioneered by figures such as Russell, Frege, Moore and early Wittgenstein. 'Wittgenstein' by Severin Schroeder (Polity Press, 2006) gives a good introduction to this 'referentialist' view of language meaning and goes on to contrast it with Wittgenstein's later view that meaning is determined by usage.

Chapter 12

[xxxix] This idea has prompted a huge amount of discussion over the centuries.

Truths of reason are sometimes referred to as 'analytic' truths. This term was coined by Kant, who came up with two definitions of analytic truth – one based on the idea of containment – that the meaning of 'unmarried' is contained in the meaning of 'bachelor'. The other definition is those truths that can be determined using this principle of contradiction. It is not obvious that these two definitions are the same, and this has resulted in much debate in the years since.

Secondly, the idea that truths of fact (termed 'synthetic' truths, by Kant) can only be established through experience and are therefore only contingently true (i.e. it might have been the case that things were different) was contested by Kant, as we saw in chapter 9. Experts largely agree that Kant's arguments for the possibility of knowledge about the world that does not come from our experience of it ('a priori' knowledge) are unconvincing and that such knowledge is impossible.

Finally, in his 1951 paper 'Two Dogmas of Empiricism' referenced above, Quine argued that even the idea of being able to neatly divide truths into truths of reason and truths of fact is ill-founded. However, perceived weaknesses in Quine's arguments have been highlighted by philosophers such as Paul Grice, P. F Strawson and H.-J. Glock and the debate continues.

xl Gödel's Incompleteness Theorem shows that for a sufficiently complex framework, there are true statements which cannot be derived from its axioms and combination rules. There are also curious self-referencing statements whose truth status is ambiguous. For example, if I am telling the truth when I say "I am lying", then I must be lying when I say "I am lying". But if I am lying when I say "I am lying", then I must be telling the truth! However, the point we are making in the section of the book, is that when working within an abstract structure (as opposed to the real world), we have all the information we need to fully bottom out whether any statement is true, false or one of these strange indeterminate cases.

For an entertaining exposition of Gödel's Incompleteness Theorem, I thoroughly recommend the renowned 'Gödel, Escher, Bach – an Eternal Golden Braid' by Douglas Hofstadter (Basic Books, 1979).

xli This amazing piece of 'post-truth' telly is available to watch on YouTube here: https://www.youtube.com/watch?v=VSrEEDQgFc8.

[xlii] The story of Fermat's Last Theorem and the quest to find a proof is marvellously told in Simon Singh's 'Fermat's Last Theorem' (Fourth Estate, 1997)

[xliii] Dewey Philip's 'Faith after Foundationalism' (Routledge, 1988) provides more on the perspective of Reformed Epistemology.

Chapter 13

[xliv] Andy Hamilton's 'Wittgenstein and On Certainty' (Routledge, 2014) provides a good exposition of the brain-in-a-vat thought experiment, as well as exploring the later Wittgensteinian thought upon which a lot of the anti-realist canon is based.

Chapter 14

[xlv] More on the Argument from Analogy and the philosophical issue of 'Other Minds' more broadly can be found at https://plato.stanford.edu/entries/other-minds/

[xlvi] A champion of this rather extreme view is American philosopher and cognitive scientist Daniel Dennett, who argued for this position in his landmark 1991 book 'Consciousness Explained' (Penguin, 1991).

[xlvii] Why not take a look at this series of videos showing lectures given by the brilliant, charming and always engaging Richard Feynman http://vega.org.uk/video/subseries/8. He talks about how hard it is to make sense of what physics tells us about world at around the 21 minute mark in this video: http://vega.org.uk/video/programme/45.

xlviii We might normally think of pain as being caused by damage to the body. It is well understood that when such damage occurs, this information is carried to the brain by pain detectors, known as nociceptors. However, it is also well understood that there are other factors involved when it comes to the amount of pain that an individual actually feels. A striking example of this is the case of a 29 year old construction worker who stepped on a seven inch nail, which went right through his boot. He was rushed to hospital in agony and sedated, but when the doctors removed the boot, they found that the nail had passed between his toes and his foot was uninjured! In a 2017 study, participants were subjected to a level of heat and then asked to rate how painful it was. At the same time, the subjects' brain activity was monitored by fMRI. The experimenters were able to correlate the level of pain reported with the fMRI scans. This meant that scientists were able to find a physical basis for the level of pain reported that went beyond what could be inferred from just the level of heat applied and nociceptor response.

Here is a link to the study mentioned, by Woo et al.: https://www.nature.com/articles/ncomms14211#MOESM1245

[xlix] xcv For more details on this, see this article from Quanta magazine: https://www.quantamagazine.org/ants-build-complex-structures-with-a-few-simple-rules-20140409/

[l] For more on free will try the Stanford Encyclopedia of Philosophy https://plato.stanford.edu/entries/freewill/

[li] The output of recent generative AI technologies has been so impressive that it even lead to Google engineer Blake Lemoine making the viral claim in 2022 that Google's LaMDA chatbot was sentient. The interview can be found online here: https://cajundiscordian.medium.com/is-lamda-sentient-an-interview-ea64d916d917

[lii] This short video from the well-known physicist Sean Carrol covers several of the different interpretations of Quantum Mechanics: https://www.youtube.com/watch?v=ZacggH9wB7Y

[liii] A thought experiment to highlight how quantum theory can lead to different observers making different claims about the world was provided by Frauchiger & Renner in their 2018 paper *Quantum theory cannot consistently describe the use of itself* which can be found here: https://www.nature.com/articles/s41467-018-05739-%208

In a slightly different formulation, Caslav Brukner also showed how quantum theory could imply different facts for different observers in his 2019 paper *A No-Go Theorem for Observer-Independent Facts* located here:
https://acrobat.adobe.com/id/urn:aaid:sc:EU:b61b5e81-8f95-46a4-8888-bfb914a968b4
An experiment to simulate the key aspects of these thought experiments is documented here:
https://www.science.org/doi/10.1126/sciadv.aaw9832

[liv] And why not finish off your investigations with this introduction to Quantum Bayesianism (QBism) located here:
https://www.youtube.com/watch?v=nSqDMtHoaTo

Index

Printed in Great Britain
by Amazon

43523033R00129